Our Stories

101

*things we know now
we wish we knew then*

**National Alliance on Mental Illness
San Diego**

in partnership with

Wisdom Legacy

This book is published by Wisdom Legacy

These are the true stories of individuals associated with the National Alliance on Mental Illness affiliate in San Diego California. These stories have been compiled from the entries of the authors to the Wisdom Legacy website, and are reprinted here pursuant to the Terms of Use governing that website where users (contributing authors) assume full responsibility for the content they contribute. All names, descriptions and details pertaining to any third parties referenced herein who are not authors have either been deleted or intentionally altered to protect the privacy of those individuals.

ISBN 978-0-578-05014-0

www.WisdomLegacy.Org

Printed in the United States of America

February, 2010

Dedication

This book is dedicated to the voices of those
individuals who could not tell their stories,
especially to the family members we have lost.

And to my brother, Jeffrey, who will always inspire
me to make change.

Mission

Our mission is to prepare people for the journey of their lives and help them make the most of the trip.

We share this mission with behavioral health, mentoring, and support organizations across America. We partner with them to achieve our common purpose. We provide a free resource to capture and share the knowledge of their organizations and a platform where the people they serve can collaborate and record the most important stories of their lives.

Our goal is to harvest from these stories the wisdom that comes from wrestling with the challenges of life and learning from the experience. We want to compile lessons about what works from 1,000,000 people, and make that knowledge available to work for those who need it. We want to break down the barriers of silence and ignorance that keep people trapped and alone. We all need to share the hope and joy that come from knowing that we are not alone, that our challenges are not unique, that solutions exist, and that all of us have both the opportunity and capability to thrive.

Our prayer is that Wisdom Legacy engages people in dialogues around the important *stuff* of life. That it serves to energize our communications and relationships; and creates an on-going and evolving commitment to each other and our descendants - a legacy and promise to our kids that the world we leave to them will be better than the world we inherited.

What do you know now
that you wish you knew then?

Please, tell us your story at
www.WisdomLegacy.org

About
NAMI San Diego

The National Alliance on Mental Illness (NAMI) San Diego is a non-profit organization whose mission is to bring hope and healing by *providing education, support, and advocacy for individuals with a mental illness, their family members, and the community at large.* Frequently, NAMI San Diego is the first point of entry into the mental health system. NAMI San Diego provides an array of support, advocacy, and education services that are free to anyone affected by mental illnesses, including: a helpline and resource center; monthly education and advocacy meetings; a 12 week Family-to-Family and 10 week Peer-to-Peer educational program; In Our Own Voice Speakers Bureau; and support groups.

NAMI San Diego services are all peer based, meaning "we have walked in your shoes, let us help guide you through this rollercoaster." This book is our shared stories of dark days, coping, recovery, and hope.

For more information, contact us at:
www.namisandiego.org or 1-800-523-5933

Table of Contents

Foreword

Over the last few months many people have been asking how Wisdom Legacy got started and how we came to partner with NAMI. For those who care about such things the following is a sumation of that story and what we have learned along the way.

Here's what happened...

Wisdom Legacy was originally conceived in 2002 as a project to capture and record stories about life's most important lessons from people who had been there--and done that-- and learned from the experience. The idea was to use the wisdom conveyed in these stories to create an on-line library of lessons learned to mentor kids and better prepare them for life. In our original vision the value of such a library would only be realized after the content was compiled. As the years have passed we've discovered that we had not understood the adventure we had begun.

The original plan to compile the library was pretty simple. In 2003 we developed a website, sought out people over 40, put one question to them, 'what do you know today that you wish you knew when you were 18,' and cataloged their responses. We tried it. It didn't work. We failed to appreciate that by 40, most people have learned so much that they can't begin to relate it all. They don't even know where to start. When faced with a generic question and a blank web page to input their answer they simply give up.

In the Spring of 2004 we started on version two. Our goal was to make the process much easier by creating the ability to ask people evocative questions about their life experiences no matter what those experiences had been. A tremendous amount of time was invested over the next few years to develop an interview-based, mentoring program called 'Please, Tell Me Your Story' that was used successfully in middle schools until 2009.

In the Spring of 2009 I reconnected with Charlie Hearn, who is on the California Board of Directors for the National Alliance on Mental Illness to show him what we were doing. He saw the applicability of our model for the mental health community. Charlie's observation was that in NAMI (as in other support orgnizations) adults mentor each other. Mentoring is at the heart of what such organizations do. Charlie suggested that we find a way to work together.

The first thing we had to do is to create an interview to address the specific issues that members of NAMI deal with everyday. We made two major enhancements to our interview process with this version. The first was suggested by a Wisdom Legacy co-founder, Dr. Heather Wood Ion, who had the idea of creating an interview which followed the path of someone's experience with mental illness from inception through to recovery or management and living with the condition. The idea essentially was to follow the life-cycle from the first moment when we see something that doesn't seem right; to the point where we realize something is actually wrong; through diagnosis; treatment; wrestling with the impacts of the condition on relationships, self-image, work and daily life; and hopefully coming out at the end in a new normal where the world is different, but you have gained some measure of control, are actively managing the condition, and are moving from being afflicted to being an advocate for yourself and others. The second enhancement came from Charlie. His suggestion was to write the questions not from the perspective of an expert researcher, but rather from the perspective of individuals and families living with mental illness who are asking for input from someone who is in the same boat.

With this new interview complete, Charlie approached a fellow NAMI California Board member, Shannon Jaccard, who happened to then be the Communication Director for

NAMI of San Diego, about running a pilot in San Diego. Shannon ran the idea past the staff and the board and shortly thereafter the pilot got underway. The book that you hold in your hands is the result of that pilot project and more than 50,000 hours of work by a team of professionals scattered across the globe.

So that's the first half—what happened.

Here's what we learned...

First, and most universally, we've found that few human encounters validate the people involved like a truly candid conversation about tackling the challenges of life. For the storyteller it's the ability to share their soul and be truly heard without the fear of being judged. When they are unexpectedly respected (rewarded) for their disclosure, they feel twice the benefit. For the listener it's the uncommon ability to receive candid advice without fear of manipulation or need to uncover a hidden agenda. For both parties it's the presence of mutual respect and trusted transparency that make the encounter so unique and valuable – even when those parties are only connected virtually through the web.

Second, it seems our interview questions are prompting people to reflect in ways rarely encountered outside of professional therapy. The questions stirred memories, brought clarity to thoughts, emotions and realizations, and prompted self-examinations that respondents reported being both deeply cathartic and surprisingly liberating. Many people have likened the process to a support group with two major differences. One, the questions are provided as a flood of evocative prompts to stir people up and get them thinking; not as one prompt at a time which may or may not resonate with a given individual. Two, in a support group, people know who you are, there are always time constraints, and there are usually others who are jockeying for 'talk time'. In this project you can be completely anonymous if you choose. You also choose the time to talk and how long you talk. A website has become a guided journal that walks participants step by step through the revelation of their own experience. The only limits in this situation are completely self-imposed.

Third, people really do learn from the challenges of life. Although we often would not have wished the things that have happened to us on anyone, looking back on it all we find that our challenges have forced us to grow in ways that we would not have grown otherwise. We realize that we've become better human beings. And we find that in spite of all we've been through we are surprisingly grateful for the growth that has come. This theme has appeared so often that we have added a section to the conclusion of this book that focuses just on the most important lessons we've learned from life – regardless of how or why we learned them.

Fourth, a frequent lament in our society has been that we recognize the worth of individuals only in terms of their capacity for economic production. This sentiment has been expressed by numerous other authors but has been brought vividly into focus through the stories of our projects. We often fail to appreciate the value of each individual's humanity. We do not do a very good job of valuing the souls of the people around us. We seem to forget how much each individual can do and become. We lose sight of the fact that each person has some spark of genius, some truly unique capacity for brilliance which too often lies hidden, unrecognized and untapped. It's as if we spend our days walking through endless fields of diamonds, but all the while think those precious stones are just glass. Sadly, we are all diminished when we fail to see these human assets and appreciate their value.

Now finally, on a personal note and along these lines, if there is anything that I'm grateful for learning from this initiative it's the growing realization that EVERYONE has something, some gift, some God given talent, some area of genius where they are brilliant. I just need to look for it, nurture it, and wait for it to present itself. Every time I meet someone now it's like a game where I'm waiting for them to show me the gift I know they've got up their sleeve. Wisdom Legacy has given me that perspective. And I've learned that the more you look, the better you get at seeing. I'm very glad I gained this appreciation. I think it's made me better with people, both as a peer, a friend, husband, father, manager. I know it has made me more grateful. When you begin to realize that your wealth is in the people who are all around you, not in the things around you, you understand just how incredibly rich you really are.

I am deeply indebted to all the hundreds of people who have taken part in the Wisdom Legacy project to date, and all who I hope will take part in the future. Your stories and lessons have had an enormous impact on me. You have been and will continue to be my own mentors. You have changed my heart, my attitude, my outlook, and my criteria for evaluating everything. For the education which I have and expect to continue to receive, I am truly and deeply grateful. I pray that others may also be so moved.

The development of this initiative and the creation of this book have been a labor of love for many people who have directly contributed to turning this dream into a reality. I hope their efforts help you to always remember that, in spite of what may seem to be evidence to the contrary, there *are answers* to your questions, and there are people out there who will help you find them.

All my best,

David P. Burrill
Chief Executive Officer
February, 2010
www.WisdomLegacy.org

14

Introduction

We knew people had stories about mental illness because we've heard so many of them in private. We knew people wanted to share their stories because they told us in NAMI surveys that it should be our highest priority. We didn't know whether people who had confronted the challenges of mental illness would be willing to step beyond the retelling of what they had experienced to examine the origins, ramifications and lessons learned from these often painful events so that their insights might be passed on to help those coming down the road behind them.

It turns out they are. This book is the result of 42 people undertaking such a project.

Mental illness, even in the mildest of manifestations, can take a devastating toll on the person with the illness and everybody close to them. NAMI exists to help those impacted by such conditions. In our work we've seen a range of reactions to the diagnosis. Some deny it. Some become defined by it. Some view it as a gift. Others stand up amid the ashes, set about the work of learning as much as they can from the events that took place, and make it their mission to get that intelligence into the hands of others who need it. These become mentors.

A mentor foresees the trials of others, appreciates that they have the power to positively affect the outcomes of those trials, and purposefully takes actions to minimize the harm and facilitate the healing of other people whom they may never know. Mentors not only help themselves to heal, they make a conscious decision to try to improve the future, and help break down the stigma of mental illness. Storytelling enables the journey from diagnosis to mentor.

This book is the work of mentors. The stories that follow trace their journey along the road of mental illness from the onset of the condition through to the time that their illness was overcome or came under management. The book concludes with a reflection on the life lessons these authors have learned from the roads they have travelled.

We believe that there are many more mentors out there who have, until now, simply lacked the platform to share what they have learned. Wisdom Legacy was created to be such a platform. This book is the first fruit of our efforts, and just the first step in a long journey of transformation. It's a great beginning, but there are millions of other equally wonderful steps along this path. Those stories are all there, right now. They're just waiting to be revealed. They're waiting for other people in other communities to come together, relate their experiences and share what they've learned.

Every time that happens we'll take one more step along the road. One more door will get opened, one more dark place will be illuminated, and we'll get one step closer to where we need to be.

Join us, won't you? Let's take another step together.

Shannon

Shannon Jaccard
Executive Director
National Alliance on
Mental Illness, San Diego
information@namisd.org

Dave

David P. Burrill
Chairman & CEO
Wisdom Legacy
dburrill@wisdomlegacy.org

Contributing Authors

Emy Alhambra

Julie Benn

–

–

Debbie Chang

Barbara Christopher

Jim Christopher

–

Ann Cummings

Theresa Dame

Jan Daughtery

Pharoh Degree

–

Maureen Dorsey

Annie Dunlop

–

James England

Devin Eshelman

–

Anita Fisher

Debbie Fox

Nancy Fuller

Brent Granado

–

Danielle Kukene Glorioso

Charlie Hearn

Julie Heinrich

–

Heather Wood Ion

Shannon Jaccard

Connie Kennemer

Kelly Levens

Christina Medrano-Huffer

Wendy McNeill

–

Rita Navarro

Bettie Reinhardt

Gloria Romero

Jean Selzer

Sally Shepherd

Diana Waugh

Lee McNeill West

Authors not wishing that their name be published are acknowledged
with a dash in place of where their name would have appeared.

About the Authors

This book has been written in an on-line collaboration between 42 unique individuals. Most of these authors do not know each other. This book is the result of a partnership between the National Alliance on Mental Illness in San Diego and Wisdom Legacy. NAMI provided most of the staffing and project coordination. Wisdom Legacy provided the technology, curriculum and project roadmap. Participants in this pilot project were primarily drawn from the staff, board, and active volunteers of NAMI San Diego. Some members of the Wisdom Legacy Initiative with first-hand experience of mental illness also participated.

Each participant has shared just a small piece of their life's story. Whether personally or as an immediate family member, each participant has experienced the challenges that mental illness visits in our lives. These stories are at once heartwrenching and hopeful. They also share remarkably consistent themes which are impossible to miss.

That such commonality should be voiced by such different people is stunning. The next several pages have been included to illustrate just how diverse this group of authors is. As you study these charts and graphs we think you will find what we have found – mental illness is not a condition of 'those people'. There is no 'them'. There is only us.

If these ensuing graphics do nothing else, they should serve to drive home the point that we are all in this together. And, if you are wondering whether there is something unique about your condition or circumstance, after reading this book, we hope you will see that you are not alone.

Gender

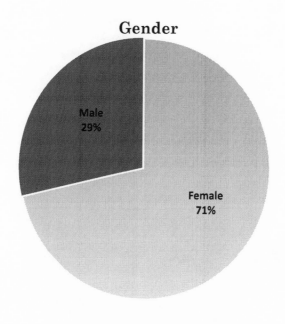

Age Range

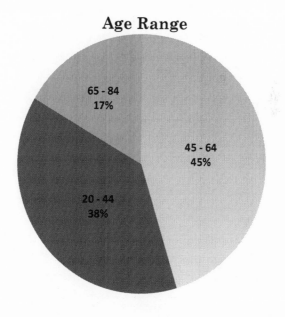

Ethnicity

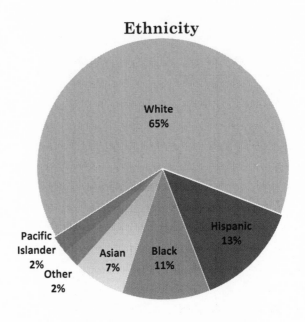

Marital Status

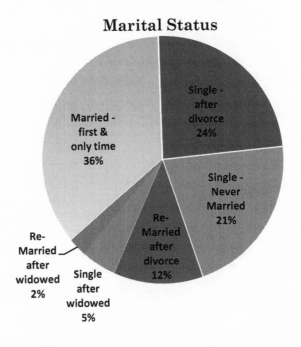

Level of Education

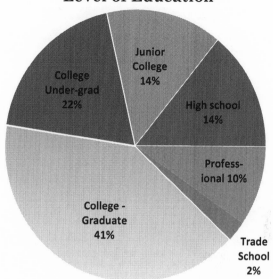

- College Under-grad 22%
- Junior College 14%
- High school 14%
- Profess-ional 10%
- College - Graduate 41%
- Trade School 2%

Parental Status

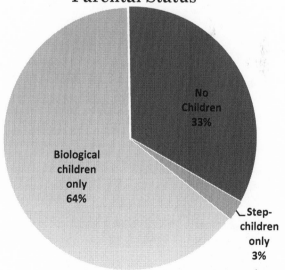

- No Children 33%
- Biological children only 64%
- Step-children only 3%

Religious Affiliation

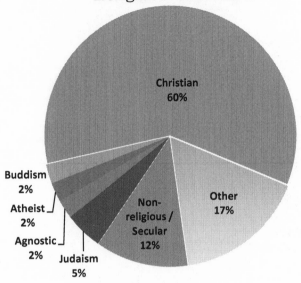

Christian
60%

Buddism
2%

Atheist
2%

Agnostic
2%

Judaism
5%

Non-religious /
Secular
12%

Other
17%

Political Perspective

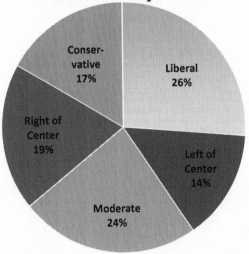

Conser-vative
17%

Liberal
26%

Right of
Center
19%

Left of
Center
14%

Moderate
24%

Industry

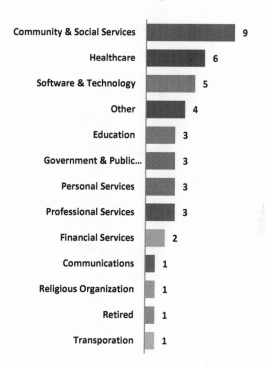

Industry	Count
Community & Social Services	9
Healthcare	6
Software & Technology	5
Other	4
Education	3
Government & Public...	3
Personal Services	3
Professional Services	3
Financial Services	2
Communications	1
Religious Organization	1
Retired	1
Transporation	1

Occupation

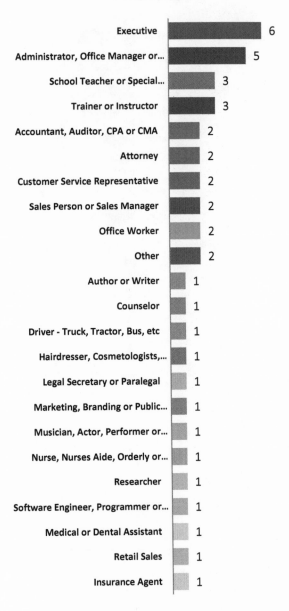

Occupation	Count
Executive	6
Administrator, Office Manager or...	5
School Teacher or Special...	3
Trainer or Instructor	3
Accountant, Auditor, CPA or CMA	2
Attorney	2
Customer Service Representative	2
Sales Person or Sales Manager	2
Office Worker	2
Other	2
Author or Writer	1
Counselor	1
Driver - Truck, Tractor, Bus, etc	1
Hairdresser, Cosmetologists,...	1
Legal Secretary or Paralegal	1
Marketing, Branding or Public...	1
Musician, Actor, Performer or...	1
Nurse, Nurses Aide, Orderly or...	1
Researcher	1
Software Engineer, Programmer or...	1
Medical or Dental Assistant	1
Retail Sales	1
Insurance Agent	1

Type of Mental Illness

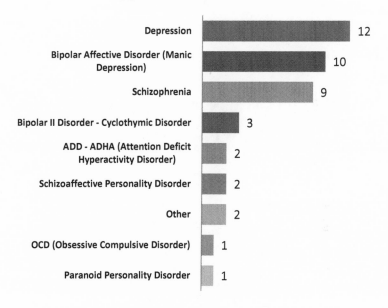

Depression	12
Bipolar Affective Disorder (Manic Depression)	10
Schizophrenia	9
Bipolar II Disorder - Cyclothymic Disorder	3
ADD - ADHA (Attention Deficit Hyperactivity Disorder)	2
Schizoaffective Personality Disorder	2
Other	2
OCD (Obsessive Compulsive Disorder)	1
Paranoid Personality Disorder	1

Relationship to Mental Illness

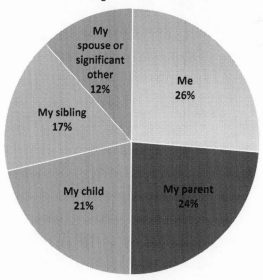

My spouse or significant other 12%
Me 26%
My sibling 17%
My child 21%
My parent 24%

Our Stories of Mental Illness

Recognition and Acceptance

Things that happened

How and when did you start to recognize that you or someone close to you had a mental illness? How old were you?

In retrospect my son was about 18 and just completed his senior year football season when he started to exhibit signs. However these signs were subtle at the time and over the next year his symptoms became worse. He became withdrawn from his family and friends and a year into his illness demonstrated very bizarre behavior. However we had no idea what we were dealing with not having any experience with mental illness. Unfortunately we had our heads in the sand.
By NAMISD.1.1b

After several trips to the emergency room and numerous medical tests, I was given a diagnosis by a neurologist of Panic Disorder. I was stunned. I had no idea what Panic Disorder was. At 32 years old and having experienced a longtime childhood illness I was no stranger to doctors and hospitals. What I felt was real. I had difficulty trying to understand that what I had originated in my brain.
By Anonymous

When I was about 21 years old I was in the United States military and I had been indulging in very severe chronic drug and alcohol abuse. I begin to get in to trouble by leaving post without permission and not showing up to work. My behavior became erratic and I quickly decompensated. I eventually was put in the brig(military prison) and that's when I first was diagnosed. I remember when I was in the cell I dissolved into a hurricane mentally, physically and spirtually. I was full of anxiety, stress, fear, and worry. I had racing thoughts and felt depressed. Then one night I heard my mother's voice call out to me out loud saying "PHAROH PHAROH WHAT HAPPENED!" At first I just kept it all to mysef but then it begain to wear me down and I asked to talk to a psychologist. After explaining to the docter about how I felt, he said that after all the indulgence and heavy chronic drug and alcohol abuse for such a long amount of time then just to stop because I was incarcerated was like "CHOPPING OFF A TAIL." Then to "COME OFF" or "COME DOWN" from the substance, it was natrual to have symptoms like hearing voices, depression, or anxiety. He also said I could of had a schizophrenic break in my brain. It was then that I was diagnosed with Drug induced psychosis. Over time other docters have diagnosed me with Schizophrenia and I have accepted that moved on with my life.

By NAMISD.1.3d

I was not aware that my son had a mental illness until he had a psychotic break. He was 30 and I was 56. He was living in Santa Barbara at the time working at Public Storage. I received a call from his landlady that he was walking naked in the neighborhood. I was stunned as he would never do a thing like that so I knew something was very wrong. My brother went with me to Santa Barbara where began days of trying to get help for him and dealing with his psychosis. When we got there, my son was in an extremely agitated state and could barely maintain. He started running saying he "needed to get rid of energy." I had to chase him down. We took him to a psychiatrist who gave us a prescription for antipsychotic medication. He said he would take it but didn't. The next day we contacted the police and found out about the PERT team. They came out with the police and, at first,

between my freshman and sophomore year because I didn't want to come home to San Diego. I was isolating away from my boyfriend, family and other friends. I couldn't understand my anxiety or depressed, sad moods. The thought of going back to school in the fall was overwhelming. This was the first time I thought seriously about suicide. At one point I actually had my hand on the bottle of pills, but then my brother called unexpectedly to tell me he was coming up to visit. That's the only reason I didn't go through with it. I started my sophomore year but the pressure, stress and depression were too much. I would have preferred to die rather than give up on my dream of graduating and becoming a coach. I didn't want to give up my scholarships as this was something I had worked on for years. Leaving school was an incredibly hard – one of the most difficult things I have ever had to do. I have tried to go back to finish my education many times but each time I have ended up in the hospital. Returning to school has proven to be just too stressful for me.

After I left Stanford I started swimming at a master's team, and moved into coaching two different teams. I also worked as a secretary. Swimming was where I met my husband. We had two children a daughter, our oldest, and then our son. I continued to suffer recurring bouts of depression over the years without ever realizing that I was actually ill. The medical profession did not pick it up. As is so often the case the people around me did not understand what they were looking at and neither did I.

Acceptance for me came after years of denial. Prozac worked to ease my depression and anxiety and brought laughter back into my life after more than a decade. I had finally been set free. The freedom was to be short lived, however, when the feelings of loss, loneliness and despair resurfaced and the ache, pain of constant worthlessness, guilt and shame returned in full force later.
By Anonymous

33

It was 1969. I was 11. My brother who was 18 months younger than I had been a 'behavior problem' in school since the third grade. By the time he was in 6th grade all hell was breaking loose. He was refusing to go to school in the morning throwing incredible tantrums that sometimes necessitated calling our family doctor to the house. He was constantly disrupting the class when he was there, and then he started to run away from school. All this was made much worse by virtue of the fact that my father was a Principal in the school district and the Principal of my brother's school was a friend / co-worker of my father. The more embarrassed my father became by his youngest sons antics the more violent the fights became as my father tried to force my brother into line.

Nothing worked. It finally got to the point where they put my bother in the hospital for a week to run tests on him to see what was going on. They found some chemical annomalies, but in 1969 they didn't have a very good sense for what that meant or what to do next.
By NAMISD.1.1a

I still cringe at the phrase mental illness and all the insidious undertones of the social stigma associated with the term. We rarely if ever hear, "I have been diagnosed with a "physical illness"…" but rather, "I have cancer…" or gout or diabetes or a heart condition or anyone of the myriad of noble physical ailments that people understand, recognize and accept. But I have a mental illness. Depression.

Recognition was a protracted and fragmented experience. Depression is sinister and subtle and forms like a creeping evening fog that settling a blackness on the heart. There was a vague awareness (not recognition) at about thirteen or fourteen years of age that something was not right. Everyone else appeared fine, happy…uninterrupted. No one seemed to be discussing having thoughts of ending their life or of whether death

34

was preferable to living with the bone crushing pain that depression brings. A cascade of events can draw you over the edge into the abyss. So first there was awareness, like hearing a distant sound and not knowing what it is.

Acknowledgment of depression is further delayed because there is an excess of deferments available for recognizing and accepting depression. As you read, you may already have started to supply some in your own mind, because no one likes depression. "All teenagers go through some down times..." or "we all have our sad times..." or "yeah, such and such happened to me (insert anything here...my cat died, my team lost, I moved, I failed an exam or whatever...) and I was bummed out. All of these...deferments...are a way of not dealing with recognition. They are the stigma associated with the disease...brought to life...acknowledge anything other than depression.

But depression is a menacing and consuming illness that left unchecked manifests itself through a multitude of bad decisions and negative behaviors. Drinking to excess, drugs, sexual indiscretion, violence (and I have lived through all of these) are not just poor choices but poor coping mechanisms to deal with the yoke of the illness. To be sure, not all people with depression live their lives in such a manner, and not all people with exhibiting these behaviors suffer from depression. Therein is the complexity of the disease, picking through and discerning that at the core of these events, for some of us, lies a debilitating illness is not easy. Moreover depression, at least in my case, was not constant but cyclical. Depression often presented itself in a slow creeping fashion that left me unaware until several days into the cycle of darkness that I was actually suffering from a bout of depression. I was in my twenties.

Recognition came slowly, by looking backwards at the debris of a life scarred. By being yet again in the same spot, down, crushed, torn apart, beaten, darkened and desiring to be alone. Tired, exhausted and without a will...there is nowhere else to face but squarely at recognizing that depression is a part of who I am. Then, more than before, things began to connect. The choices, pains and evidence was more clear. I was in my thirties by this point and realized I had survived but carried a heavy burden, which I often spilled onto others in my life. There was a reason for some of the emotional detritus in my life. Depression.

Acceptance...is another journey...I am still working it out.
By Anonymous

It was the early 1980s. Our son was 19, attending Community College, working part time in retail and playing the drums in a very successful young band. He was heavily invested in all three of these activities, and enjoying each one. We became aware of changes in his behavior. He began to show signs of paranoia and to suspect people were against him in all of these environments. He began to isolate from everyone except the family. We were in our mid forties and were in the middle of relocating to another city and state due to a job promotion. His two sisters, both attending university, were making plans to cope with the move, but he seemed unable to make the necessary adjustment, did not come up with a plan, so moved with us. It was not until the florid symptoms of responding to voices that we did not hear, and writing incoherent scribblings, that we became aware that he needed professional help.
By Anonymous

I was 31 years old when I finally recognized my younger brother Brother was depressed. I use the word "finally" because my guess is that he struggled with depression his entire life—so unfortunately it took me 20 plus years to see it. Recognizing my brother's mental illness was something that I did too little too late. In fact, my life's greatest regret is not recognizing the signs earlier, not seeing that he was struggling, not reaching out and protecting him before it was too late.

The tragic ending to this story is that I didn't recognize that was brother was depressed in time to help him--in time to make a difference and save his life. Sadly, I didn't recognize my brother was suffering with depression until the moment I learned of his death by suicide. It rips me apart to think of the years he must have suffered in silence not to mention the pain he must have felt the hours before he made the desperate decision to take his own life. All of this was happening inside my brother his entire life and I didn't see it. While suicide is certainly a term I was familiar with I never really thought it could touch my life, touch my family, or most importantly, touch my brother. What I have learned through this entire experience is that suicide doesn't discriminate and that suicide is far more people than I ever thought have been touched by suicide one way or another in their life.
By Anonymous

What were the behaviors or symptoms that caught your attention?

It became obvious that my husband had no comprehension of the consequences of his own actions. He would say things without realizing that they were cruel, would do things which had a great impact on others, such as forgetting the class he was to teach, and then would not understand why others were distressed. This ranged from the trivial--losing keys, or having to try on a dozen different shirts before one 'looked right' having pulled the previous 11 off violently removing the buttons, to major-- such as not showing up for work.
By Anonymous

There were many. He became withdrawn from family and

37

turned off friends completely . He would stay in his room when we were home except when we went to bed. While we were at work he would move furniture all over the house. He would make bizarre arts and crafts items. He would use anything in the garage to build things that had no practical use. Hygiene became a major problem which at one point even turned into making an outhouse for he refused to use the bathroom. He would "decorate" our cars at night with torn up boxes and newspapers.

By NAMISD.1.1b

I once heard a family member describe the inital impact of symptoms in their family member's mental illness was like watching a switch turned to "off" and the person that once existed just vanished. I have often racked my brain for earlier signs and signals of the onset of this illness, but despite vague concerns, no red flags ever surfaced. Instead on a night in my son's junior year of high school, while studying for the SAT college boards, I found him hunched over his books, comatose, with saliva slowly dripping onto his materials. From that sentinel moment forward, symptoms seem to occur in quick sucession. Our son became a recluse, enclosed in his room, often his bed, and always inside himself. Our once vibrant teenager so alive with love for life seemed incapable of even smiling.

Concentration and abilitity to complete small tasks seemed like a herculean effort. Calls and visits from friends went unanswered and school once adored became too difficult to navigate. Basically we saw our beloved son pull away from his very life. Talks of suicide were frequent and visits to medical doctors for a host of ongoing symptoms were frequent. Self medication through alcohol and drugs in subsequent years became another important behavior too important to ignore. Any stressful event whether in personal or school life became unbearable and resulted in an increase in symptoms. These were the the symptoms and behaviors we noticed.

By Anonymous

I literally could not see straight!! My vision was fuzzy and I felt as if I was suffocating!
By Anonymous

I remember feeling extremely happy, energized, like I was on top of the world. It was a like a drug, and I became addicted to that "up" feeling. I also remember experiencing the lows and seeing myself not want to see the light of the day.
By Anonymous

As a young adult, I wasn't well versed in psychiatric terminology and the various mental illnesses. In fact, I don't know that I even knew what major depressive disorder was. I do know that growing up my brother never really seemed happy. Sadly, the clues were always there, I just didn't look hard enough for them. We noticed problems with my brother that we so lovingly termed "anger management" problems.

My brother was a brilliant boy with so much going for him. Unfortunately, a learning disability, some very cruel children and a few not so patient teachers wore on my brother's spirit. By the time he was in 5th grade he developed a tough exterior. He became a fighter—if he was going to go through this life then he was going to be tougher than all of the people that belittled him. It was his protective factor-his shield from the pain of others.

Unfortunately, living as a fighter came at an expense as it wore on Brother's spirit to keep such a façade going. He was a naturally kind, loving boy deep down so playing the tough guy became exhausting at times. So, it was around 5th grade when life just started to become too much for Brother. People made him feel dumb and he often wondered if they were right. Going to school became a struggle, making friends was difficult, and he no longer had an interest in pursuing the things that he once enjoyed like sports and other hobbies.

We began to notice him withdrawing from the things he normally loved—he no longer had an interest in participating in the things he once loved. This should have been the first big and clear sign for us that something serious was wrong. But, we missed it—we just couldn't articulate that his behavior could be a result of depression.

As time went on Brother became very angry. He was angry at the world, and angry at everyone and everything. My family and I would tiptoe around him because we didn't want him to explode at us. I now see that his anger was a representation of the pain he was feeling inside, a representation of the deep loneliness and the overwhelming despair that he had.

I now see that depression is an illness that will ravage the soul—it will eat up every ounce of happiness and joy that a person has and make life so unbearable that the only option out, for some, is death. Sadly, at a young age of 27, that was the option that my darling brother chose.
By Anonymous

What impact did these behaviors have on you and your family?

My behavior had a huge impact on me and my family. I ended up strung-out on drugs and alcohol, in jails and prisons, homeless. Myself or my family didn't know what to do. We were in turmoil. It was hard for me to get my life back on track. It took 10 long hard years.
By NAMISD.1.3d

At first we were very scared of not knowing what was

happening or knowing the reason why he was acting this way, then we where embarrased, we lost many friends and acquaintances, and ended up moving from the area where we grew up. For the longest time we couldn't talk about it outside the home. It was kept a secret from others. I personaly couldn't talk about it. I would cry every time someone touched the subject. I basically then became my brother's advocate and managed his money & wrote his checks and drove him around. I was only about 13 years old. Looking back that is a big reasponsibility. I just did it because he was my brother & I loved him. I was also very proud that he had the courage to go to the Army, and mad as hell against those people that beat my brother for no reason and got away with it. They moved on to have children, work, among other things, and my brother has really no life. He's always in secluded places, can't be around too many people for long periods of time, won't be able to have kids or get married because a lot of women wouldne't be able to deal with his illness. I'm very sad for my brother. He lost many, many friends. It was like he had leprosy or something like it.

By grome_420

We always believed our son would be okay. He had something that presented a problem with him taking on life like the rest of us. I could never quite connect with the diagnosis. He continued to love to do things - golf, fishing, skateboarding, going to the movies, piano...

We kept pushing him to work and to go to school. Both were difficult and he did them for short periods of time, on and off.

We were very involved in our son's life almost like looking for the cure and we were ready to do the next thing.

By BC

Without question my brother's depression impacted my entire family. Since my brother's depression often manifested in the shape of anger, when he was really low he had a presence that was, at times, intimidating. We didn't know what the right thing to say or do when he was angry so we found ourselves tiptoeing around him during family dinners, family vacations, sporting events, and holidays. While I loved my brother deeply his depression certainly got in the way of our ability to connect and to bond.

What complicated it for me, as a sibling, was that my mother was always worried about Brother so she was constantly doting over him trying to keep him safe and happy. While I now see that as a parent that was absolutely the right thing to do, as the older sibling, I sometimes resented all of the love and attention he got. Even worse was that since I didn't struggle with depression myself I often, very selfishly, felt as though he should just get over it--just pull himself up by his bootstraps and stop being so cranky and bringing me down.

I wish I had known then what depression was. I wish I had the knowledge or the education to understand that what my brother was experiencing wasn't a choice—it was an illness. My brother had a very serious and life threatening illness that required doctors' care and attention—and he never got that care or attention. I can't help but feel, on some level, that my inability to empathize and help him only exacerbated the problem. My hope is that I can use my story to reach out to others and help them recognize the signs and symptoms of depression before it is too late because while depression is a serious illness it does not have to be an illness that takes lives.

By Anonymous

Was the realization that you were dealing with mental illness sudden and traumatic or a slow evolution? If it took a while, how long did it take and what caused the delay?

It was a slow process and only became obvious days before he walked through a glass door. Even after a 5150 I relied on hope rather than acknowledge the severity of the illness. The delay was caused by a combination of being in unfamiliar territory and denial.
By NAMISD.1.1b

The realization that I had a mental illness did not happen until after I was paralyzed from a suicide attempt. On April 5, 2003, I leaped off a three story balcony of a sober living home in Los Angeles. I don't remember any details because it was so traumatic, yet before that I was struggling with my own marijuana addiction which masked the real problem: mental illness. For years I was in denial to the fact at the same time seeing private psychologists, psychiatrists, and even taking medication unfaithfully for about two years. Once the drug addiction was cured from over a month's stay in a treatment facility, my mind needed something else to lean on in order to deal with the Bipolar symptoms. The temporary answer was suicide until I finally acted on my thoughts and feelings. When I was in the rehab hospital this time as a paraplegic I knew that I needed help and there were doctors to give me the correct diagnosis and treatment.
By NAMISD.1.4h

I'd say my life was the realization. It was a tornado. It took 10 long years and the delay was my addiction to drugs and alcohol.
By NAMISD.1.3d

My recognition of my clinical depression, and the recognition of my friends and family, was a slow evolution. It took about five months before a friend, who was an occupational therapist, said she thought I had

clinical depression. The delay was caused by none of us knowing about clinical depression or recognizing it.
By Anonymous

In spite of my medical training, I really didn't know any more about mental illness than the names of the disorders. After some very difficult moments at work with a verbally abusive director of surgery, I had a panic attack (although at the time I thought I was having and M.I.) I was admitted to my own hospital and had many tests, but nothing was found. But after 3 or so months of feeling constantly exhausted and unwilling to do anything, I went to my own doctor. Thankfully, he sat down and really listened. He said "It sounds like there is some depression here." He prescribed some anti-depressants and told me to find a therapist. I saw her for about six months before I began to peruse websites and blogs, and decided that it (depression) sounded just like me.

At the time, I didn't know that depression affected many individuals in my extended family. One day, around that time, I was so miserable that I felt like taking all the pills in the bottle. I told my doctor, and he arranged for me to see a psychiatrist the very next day. I was admitted to the hospital several times during those first few years, but I still refused to believe that I was really that sick. I always felt guilty - that my illness was not severe enough to be compared with others. However, as treatments came and went, (I even agreed to have ECT, but that did not help - and it left me with severe memory loss) I began to realize that I really had a problem, and that treating it was going to be very difficult..
By bookit1

Actually it was a relief to know that there was a label then treatment for what I had. I had never heard the term Mental Illness and didn't know that depression, anxiety and panic attacks were treatable disorders.

I had been in therapy through Employee Assistance Programs since my Mother's suicide in 1969. She was never diagnosed or treated and it wasn't until my father's suicide in 1995 that I went into a deep depression and was diagnosed with major Depression. The meds I was put on shot me into mania and I was re-diagnosed with Bi-Polar, added diagnosis of PTSD in 97 then ADHD in 2008.

I think Shame, Ignorance and Guilt prevented me from getting the treatment I needed. I think I was good at covering up- I thought I was a weak person and afraid that I would be "put away" if I told all that I was doing and feeling. Also, I was a manager for a large Govt. Contractor and I was afraid of losing my high security clearance which was required for my job.

Also I never saw the same person over six months which was allowed on the EAP. Also, they were contracted for one year only. One Psychiatrist thought my bizarre sleeping and spending habits were just coping strategies against the depression.
By NAMISD.1.4c

Cockroaches at Rockbottom
The realization that I had a mental illness occurred when I received a diagnosis of bipolar disorder at age 19. The acceptance of this disorder was much harder to come by and didn't happen until I was 29, and that was only after hitting rockbottom. It was then that I took responsibility for my illness and began my recovery.

The trajectory of my illness of bipolar happened in a textbook fashion. I went up; I went down. I went up; I went down. I went up; I went down. The type of bipolar disorder I had was more severe on the manic side, so I was accustomed to being hospitalized annually for weird, strange, and often dangerous behavior. It was not unusual for me to come into contact with the PERT (Psychiatric Emergency Response Team), a specialized branch of the the police department, and end up in handcuffs on my way to the hospital. I went through this routine for ten years. I spent on the average a month and a half on an inpatient unit almost every year during my 20's.

There were many reasons for my delayed embrace of the disorder.

My manic states, in their infancy, were purely euphoric and were kicked off by a period of hypomania, or "mild" mania. During these periods, I was full of positive energy that was in the bounds of normalcy and interpreted as "charisma," "drive," and "fun." I worked hard; I played hard. I held down a regular job and moonlighted as a swing dance teacher, making a decent living. I was well-liked and "extremely energetic," the precursor for the explosive manias that were inevitably to follow.

During the periods of mania, I didn't eat or sleep, and ran around like a banshee. I spent time "with God" and would often hallucinate, sometimes about the Garden of Eden, sometimes about the resurrection of dead loved ones, sometimes about "the interconnectedness of the universe." Bottom line, though, the manic experience was heady, fearless, creative, and trippy. I felt things on a "higher level," and despite the horrible aftermath, I was still besotted with the mania. When I came back to "normal," I was just waiting for my high energy to come back so I could "get stuff done" and "be fun again." It was not a recipe for self insight.

Eventually, though, the manias started to sour. The mania and the depression started to coalesce into "mixed-states," and new symptoms like profound anger began to seep in. I decimated a few key relationships. One young man I dated, when I was in the midst of a manic episode, thought I was going to kill him. But the turning point was a post-hospitalization trip to Mexico with a morally disturbed individual. I lived in Tijuana for two months, often without even basic necessities like food.

46

When I returned home, my mother decided to put me in a board and care called the Orangewood Manor.

Orangewood was a warehouse for the mentally ill, 44 people residing there in a ramshackle complex. Some residents had been there for as many as 15 years. It was a step away from being homeless, and I was going to be there until I got a job and could move out on my own, per my mother's orders.

Orangewood was bitterly depressing. The dirt courtyard was decorated with rusty, metal folding chairs, rustier, jumbo coffee cans for ashtrays, and withering rose bushes. A grainy, ancient television was always on in the day room with comatose people clustered around it for hours on end on filthy mismatched couches. The food was hardly edible. Thankfully, my room was decently sized, and I lucked out on the roommate situation because Susan was a sweetheart, tall, red-headed, and schizophrenic, with only occasional but predictable delusions. We got along great.

It was at Orangewood that I got the turn.

There wasn't much to do. I ate, I slept, I watched Frasier down the hall on my friend's dubious television. In general I subsisted quite well, although shame and despair were always in my heart. My one pastime that was not shared by anyone else was reading. I took it upon myself to get a library card and proceeded to read books on the Holocaust, as I have always had a passion for stories of human survival in worlds of utter depravity and evil.

Late one night I was reading "Sophie's Choice" by William Styron. After a particularly dark section, I felt compelled to put the book down. I looked at the clock, an old, digital, dinosaur type given to me by my "boyfriend" as a Valentine's present, and it was past 4:00 am. I did a double-take, aghast, as I saw a roach crawling in THE INSIDE of the clock. Then, to my absolute horror, I looked

47

at the top, the "speaker," and saw a colony of baby roaches dodging in and out of the little holes.

I sprang up in bed, as if from a bad dream. "Why am I here?" I screamed in my head, "Why am I here? I don't belong here!" My own inner voice answered, "You're here because you have a mental illness. You have a mental illness. It's not your fault. You have a mental illness."

I have to say this was the first time I had ever had a heart-to-heart with myself about having a mental illness. Before, I had framed my disorder in terms of "something artists have," or "a genetic disorder," or "something that makes me interesting and special." I never really thought of the illness as...well...an illness. For me, I had to be stripped of nearly everything that was dear to me to be able to have the clarity to figure out that I had a problem.

Once that job was done, the real job began...
By NAMISD.1.6h

What made you finally seek help?

I don't say I sought help but help sought me. My family and GOD brought me to the realization that sobriety, medicaiton, and counseling was the life I had to live if I wanted to stay free from destruction.
By NAMISD.1.3d

I had to give up my jobs, I couldn't support myself, and I could no longer function in daily life.
By Anonymous

What were the reactions of your family and friends?

48

Our situation resulted in a very serious crime being committed which has traumatized our family. Aside from us as parents there are 3 siblings. The entire effects of the illness and resulting crime are profound and probably not fully understood. After 8 years each of us cope in our ways. Some better than others.
By NAMISD.1.1b

The reactions to the discovery that my son had Schizophrenia were varied. My husband (not the father of my son) and I separated almost immediately because I knew the unsympathetic, hostile atmosphere in our house would be detrimental to my son's mental health. We divorced and my son and I have lived together for the last 12 years. I am happy about this decision, not only because I was able to provide a loving, caring home for my son but because it was something that needed to happen for my good as well.

On the other hand, my two brothers stepped up to the plate unreservedly doing what was needed for my son. My son's breakdown took place in Santa Barbara and one of my brothers went there with me where we spent a week trying to get help for him. We could write a book about our experiences during that time, dealing with the police, a psychiatrist, the hospital, and my son himself. I will never forget what my brother did for me because, otherwise, I would have been alone, facing a daunting ordeal. After my son was admitted to the hospital, my brother went home and my other brother came up for several days to help pack up my son's belongings for the trip home and to be a support to me and to him.

My friends were sympathetic even though they did not understand what mental illness meant any more than I did.
By NAMISD.1.5d

Once our son was diagnosed and news spread of the

mental illness, I was surprised to notice that family and friends had become very quiet and my son's friends suddenly disappeared. When this happened I found it helpful for my son to take him for rides to the beach and stay around him daily. It was not always easy but it did help my son "stay in the moment."
By drive1

How did you feel after reality sunk in?

At first I felt angry and worried. But I soon realized that I would rather be known throughout the whole world as someone who is clean, sober and med-compliant, then someone who is on drugs and in and out of prison.
By NAMISD.1.3d

I felt extremely scared and hopeless.
By Anonymous

Sadly, I didn't learn of my brother's depression until it was too late--until I learned of his suicide. So, I was left to put the pieces together and try to understand my brother's illness while also grieving. It has been a dark and sad road for me because not only do I have the grief associated with losing someone so important to me but I also have all of the questions that arise when someone takes their own life.

What I have come to see is that suicide is insidious--and it will literally rip apart the people that are left behind to make sense of it. Not a single day goes by that I don't wonder what I could have done differently--what I could have done to save him--what clues I might have missed in the days leading up to his death. It is a painful, lonely road to grieve a loved one--and it is especially complicated to grieve that loved one when you realize that they chose death over life.

I spend my days thinking about what those final moments must have felt like for him. Did he feel peace? Did he feel scared? Did he think we would be better off without him? Did he really understand the finality of his decision? Did he know that I loved him? Intellectually, I realize that I will never know the answers to these questions. However, in order for me to truly accept and heal the loss of my brother I realize that my journey must include a path towards accepting, truly accepting, that I will never know the answers to these questions and that is OK.
By Anonymous

Is there anything else that has happened to you or that you've experienced in this area that you would like to share?

I learned that 1 in 5 people will experience mental illness in their lifetime. Almost 20 million every year. Life happens....we loose a job, a spouse, a child, we experience a serious illness. Any of these can trigger an episode of of mental illness.
By Anonymous

Things you learned

In hindsight is there anything you wish you would have spotted or acted upon sooner?

There is plenty. If armed with the knowledge I have now I would have sought professional help in the early stages. The illness became so severe that getting through to my son to visit a physician became impossible. I saw

everything I just did not know what it was or what to do about it.
By NAMISD.1.1b

Yes, most definitely. Over six and a half years ago before my suicide attempt, I did not know I was not alone when I was uncomfortable in the symptoms of either mania or depression. I was unaware of any support groups or day programs I could attend to relate with others who really understood where I was coming from. I wish I knew that the places I was so fragile on the inside could have turned into opportunities to strengthen myself or others. Furthermore, how to be comfortable with myself in the months prior to my suicide attempt did not have to be as difficult. Fortunately, now I know what to do with the reoccurring symptoms which I will try and outline here.

First, mindfulness. I can tune the negative thoughts out and concentrate on the vitality of my breath (or something else). This practice allows me to be OK with the pain and experience moments of peace and tranquility.

Second, bettering my relationship with God. I cannot think of a better way to renew my mind than through the Bible. Romans 10:17 reads the following, "Consequently, faith comes from hearing the message, and the message is heard through the word of Christ."

Third, the 5 Recovery Pathways are now outlets for me to go to first heal myself and then help others. They include hope, choice, empowerment, recovery environment, and spirituality (meaning and purpose). I learned these by taking the Peer Employment Training offered by Recovery Innovations.
By NAMISD.1.4h

I wish I would have come to the knowledge of sobriety. I

wish I would have come to the grips of the fact that a drug and alcohol free life would have been healthier for me.
By NAMISD.1.3d

No, because I needed to experience what I went through to the get me to the position I am at today. I used to regret the past alot, but once I began talking about my illness with others I saw it in a different light and this helped.
By Anonymous

Was there anything or anyone that helped you come to grips with this condition? If so, what did they do?

As a person who believes in both faith and traditional medicine, I sought advice and treatment from both. It was life changing to learn that what I had was a medical condition and would be treated as such. I also learned my illness was not my fault, sign of personal weakness, lack of faith or willpower. I also learned from a Christian perspective what God had to say about me and my illness. As a result my faith became stronger, and I learned to define myself by what and who God says I am, not by the opinions of persons ignorant to the truths about mental illness. I learned from other Christians who had experienced mental illness that God had a purpose and plan for my life and that having a mental illness was not a disqualification to receiving all that God has planned for my life and future. No condemnation, but plans for a future with filled with hope an unconditional love.
By Anonymous

I say GOD and my family helped me come to grips with my conditon. Their LOVE and persistant support carried me through. Like it says in the book of Hebrews chapter

13 verse 5 from The Holy Bible.....''for he hath said, I WILL NEVER LEAVE THEE, NOR FORSAKE THEE.''
By NAMISD.1.3d

Unintentional Angel
The person who helped me tremendously in coming to grips with my bipolar diagnosis had no idea he was doing it.

One of the key pieces in my recovery was my participation in a support group, DBSA, the Depression and Bipolar Support Alliance. At the very beginning of my involvement, I had an inkling that if I changed my lifestyle, I could stop being victimized by the symptoms of my illness. I had an inkling with a dash of hope, but that was all. After all, I had had major episodes once a year since the onset of my illness--a decade's worth--and I was used to them. I didn't have any tangible evidence that life could be any other way.

Then I met Doug. Doug was at first glance a "normal guy." He looked like a good dad. Always dressed like a golfer, Doug had a vestige of an East Coast accent, being from Massachusetts. He was warm, kind, and mellow. I had him pegged for someone in the DBSA "parents group," there to support a child with mental illness.

As it turns out, although Doug had a daughter with bipolar, I learned that he had bipolar disorder himself. I was blown away. He didn't look the part; he didn't act the part, and he had "a life." He was comfortably retired, happily married, and enjoyed playing golf. He was calm and affable. Most important, he hadn't had an episode in eight years. Eight years!

Over time, I cultivated a friendship with Doug. I don't think he realized that our "chance" interactions were not chance at all, but a deliberate effort on my part to learn his "secret." His secret, as it turns out, amounted to common sense in recovery, common sense that was beyond my power to implement overnight, but common sense nonetheless. He advised me to go to bed at the same time every night, wake up at the same time every day, eat healthy food on time, exercise, get sun, forgo alcohol, and spend time with positive people.

Wow! It would take me a thousand years to do all those things, particularly since I was still embedded in a dysfunctional lifestyle, but a least I had a road map that I trusted. Hearing such advice from a therapist was nothing like hearing it from the horse's mouth. Plus, I had proof that his formula worked, proof right before my very eyes.

Doug eventually moved to Arizona to be near his daughter, but he left behind the memory of a positive role model. Because of Doug's influence on my life, I learned that sometimes all it takes is listening to someone who has been there and being determined to follow suit. Doug also taught me that to have a positive impact on someone else, it doesn't require Herculean effort, but occasionally the chance remark, or just being there. After all, "80% is just showing up." In Doug's case, all he did was show up, but without even knowing it, he made an indelible mark on my life. Now I can say it's been eight years since I've had a major episode. Eight years!
By NAMISD.1.6h

If there were a long delay from the onset of the symptoms to the acknowledgement of the illness, what were the consequences of that delay?

The consequences were severe. A life was taken and two families were changed forever.
By NAMISD.1.1b

In that year, my Social Security record shows that I made 1/4 of what I usually earn during the year. So my ability to perform a job and my income were severely impacted.
By Anonymous

I had many years of fear and anguish. I lost my career, my home, my relationship with friends and family and my self respect.
By NAMISD.1.4c

Once you had acknowledged the condition, what was the most important or positive thing that you did to deal with it?

Once acknowledging that our son was indeed struggling with mental illness, the single most positive thing we did was to admit our son needed help and seek optimal psychiatric assistance. While I assumed this would be an easy step, it was anything but. Initial attempts led to frustrating office visits resulting in poor quality of care and limited ability for positive interactions with either my son our my husband and myself. It wasn't until over seven years later we found a wonderful psychiatrist that led to a definite diagnosis . Thankfully, we were introduced to a truly talented and caring psychologist. Slowly he won our son's trust and help him begin baby steps to recovery.

Obviously medication was another important need, but since that is an inexact science that also took many years before the correct "cocktail" of medications for our son was discovered.
By Anonymous

I contacted NAMI to get all the information I could about Schizophrenia since I did not know a single thing about it.

They were extremely helpful, especially the volunteers I spoke to who had been through this themselves. I desperately needed to know that there was hope for my son and I found it with them. I read everything I could get my hands on about this illness so that I could give my son the best chance for recovery. This is so important because it has been found that mentally ill people do so much better with a loving, understanding family. But one needs to be educated about the illness in order to provide the best environment for them. For instance, people with Schizophrenia can't tolerate a loud, noisy, abrasive, critical environment and, if the family learns this, they can adapt their behavior so that it helps the person with the illness.

By NAMISD.1.5d

What's the difference between acknowledging mental illness and accepting it?

The difference is time. Acceptance takes time. It's almost like dealing with the stages of grief. Denial, Anger than after awhile acceptance. I was very angry I was no longer the person who could do everything! I wanted her back! Denial, there was NO way I Had "That" illness. But I did and I learned I was not to blame for my illness. It's not because I was weak or lacked character. Learning it wasn't my "fault" set me free from feeling guilty to concentrate on getting well.

By Anonymous

I think the difference between acknowledging mental illness and accepting it is acknowledging you have a mental illness is simply believing it. Accepting it is being compliant with the steps and the life of recovery.

By NAMISD.1.3d

I think that acknowledging that one has a mental illness is a gigantic step. For me, that step brought a lot of fear that I would never get better, and my life would deteriorate even more drastically. Once I got better finally, I went off my medication in several months. The recurrence of the severe depression caused me to attempt suicide. After getting better a second time, I think I then accepted that severe depression was something that I was susceptible to, and that if I didn't want to have the horrible consequences, I needed to keep taking medication, recognize warning signs, and do everything I could to stay out of it, which I have done successfully for almost 20 years.
By NAMISD.1.4i

Acknowledging my illness and accepting it were two very different moments. For years I felt guilty about my weakness - maybe this was all my fault, maybe I wasn't as sick as all that. I even used to ask my therapist: "Is my depression really that severe, compared to other people's?" I lost many friends when I lost my job, so I didn't really have anyone to compare notes with. As I tried a long series of different medications that either never worked or only worked temporarily, I began to be afraid that I was never going to get better. By this time I had learned about the multitude of family members who either suffered from depression or bi-polar disorder - even my own mother, who never told me. At times I wanted to hurt myself, or run away - but I never considered suicide - I felt that I could never do that to my family.

I knew that I could never work full-time again, so I got involved with NAMI San Diego, which was truly life-saving. I must admit I had a lot of anger in me - about losing my job, my friends, about the difficulty my husband had in coping with me. I think what finally kept me going was a sense of anger about the treatment of the mentally ill. I became a very staunch advocate, and spoke publicly at every opportunity I got. I finally came to "accept" my illness about 5 years into it, when I accepted that this would be with me forever, and that instead of constantly mourning the loss of my old life, I needed to pattern my new life based on the limitations imposed by my symptoms (stress, fatigue, anxiety, unbelievable sadness at times, self-isolation...). I was still the very bright person that I used to be, but I had to organize my life so that I could still accomplish the goals that I had set without aggravating my illness.

I have never felt intimidated or ashamed about talking to others about my illness - how else will people learn to understand what mental illness is and what it isn't? Acceptance is not always an easy attitude to maintain, as the course of chronic treatment-resistant depression is full of ups and downs - but I try to "turn fear into generosity," as someone said, by helping others to learn what I had learned.

By bookit1

The
Mental Healthcare
Delivery System

Things that happened

What were your experiences as you navigated the mental healthcare delivery system?

When I went to the first MD, he prescribed an older antidepressant, Desyrel, because I didn't think I could afford Prozac, which was newly out. This particular MD was not at all helpful about talking to me about depression. Desyrel got me up off the floor, but just barely. I did find a psychologist, who was very helpful in telling me about depression and helping me to understand myself. However, I still was not getting well. My daughter found an inpatient clinic in Washington, D.C., the Minerth-Meier-Byrd clinic, which does not exist as such anymore. After much persuasion, I finally allowed myself to be taken by my daughter to D.C. from California and checked in there. My daughter had also convinced my current employer, where I was not able to function on the job, to keep me on the rolls and on health insurance for several more months. Dr. B., the psychiatrist in charge, talked to me for at least two hours to convince me to try Prozac. After two weeks there, I was better, but not able to function on the outside yet. My insurance would not approve any more time in the clinic. So Dr. B. said that if I could stay with my parents, which I did, I could be treated for free as an outpatient for another two weeks. After that, I still was not ready to go home to California and find a job and resume my life. So I stayed with my parents for another couple of weeks, seeing my therapist from the clinic about 3 times a week. After another two weeks, I woke up one morning, and was feeling good and ready to go home.

In California, I found another psychiatrist, whom I kept for many years, and now am treated by my MD, knowing that if I need to I will go back to a psychiatrist. I also continued with my psychologist when I returned home until she and I thought I no longer needed her. My psychiatrists and MDs were paid by my insurance, but my psychologist was not. She allowed me to pay as I could and what I could. I am extremely grateful to all the health care professionals and my family who helped me along the way. I'm not very grateful to my insurance company at the time, because it prevented me from getting the medication or care I needed in a timely manner.

By NAMISD.1.4i

Our son's behavior suggested he might need a rehab facility. We learned about a place for men (our son was only 18), where prayer and sacrifice was a big focus. It was an out of state facility. We were called by them to come pick him up. They noticed some odd behavior and believed he needed some other help. We were helpless and did not understand. Upon picking our son up, we noticed he seemed a "little off." We did not understand and expected him to get better.

We were lost! Lots of crying and confusion and what to do surrounded every moment of each day. I don't know how, but in speaking to others, we got the name of the first psychiatrist who saw our son. He was older and saw our son about 2 times. He put him on an antipsychotic - which we also knew nothing about. He said we lived too far away and that our son wasn't getting anything out of seeing him so we were left 'out in the cold.'

Our son complained of headaches from this medication, so taking it didn't last long. I remember taking him to a therapist, (and then of course there is the cost). We didn't understand what was happening, we wanted to help our son, but there were no instructions to help us. We even took him to a doctor in San Francisco and even though his fees were exorbitant, I think we would have tried to work with him more, but his secretary allowed the blood draw to get warm, and therefore useless, and trying to manage from S.D. became too difficult for us to figure out. I became obsessed with reading about Schizophrenia and antipsychotics.

Our son just didn't fit this category; in some things maybe, but just in some. We took our son to another prominant physician in S.D. I don't know how we got his name. We had one meeting with him. He decided that our son had Schizophrenia because he could not explain the expression "A bird in the hand is worth two in the bush." This was odd to us. He also put our son back on the medication that gave our son bad headaches. We just didn't get this and he wasn't very willing to explain. He basically didn't want to see us again. Then I meet a woman who had a Schizophrenia diagnosis and was now well for over 15 years. We went to her doctor. He is a young people's psychiatrist. He was warm, friendly, and cautious in his use of medication. (He understood my concerns about medication.)

Our son went out to "have some fun." He ended up in the psychiatric ward. We wanted to get him some help for the mental illness and the alcohol, but trying to get him into a facility seemed another trial. I am not sure we or the doctor had the right information. Our son's stay in the hospital grew longer and our son was pushed off on another doctor who got him into a different hospital and with the choices of the doctor and the staff our son's life was taken from him.
By BC

How are you currently treating this condition?
How has that changed over time?

I take medication faithfully. I see a Psychiatrist every three months. I have found meds with few side effects, but I need to I use cognitive therapy and meditation and watch my sleep and stress.

When I first started my treatment it was only medication- about a year later I started group. I took cognitive therapy about three years ago. I don't do formal group, but I have friends who either have the illness or family members I talk to and see a therapist if needed.
By NAMISD.1.4c

Which treatments worked well? Which haven't worked at all?

Desyrel didn't work much at all; Prozac has worked extremely well for almost 20 years. My psychiatrists, psychologists, and current MD have been extremely helpful. In addition to mental health professionals and medication, I have found that Co-Dependents Anonymous helped me enormously. There I learned how to have healthy relationships with myself and others. Also, from my therapists, I have learned to modify my "stinking thinking" and behavior. Spiritual direction has also helped me a lot in being able to turn my anxieties and stresses over to God.
By NAMISD.1.4i

What was the original prognosis and what is the prognosis now? How has that prognosis affected you?

That's an interesting question. I wasn't really given a prognosis. I was told I had a mental illness and I would have to take medication the rest of my life. Since my first medications had so many side effects I thought I would always feel bad.

Today my prognosis is that living in recovery is great....Doesn't mean it's always wonderful..I still have bad times if get too little sleep or stressed, but I have tools and don't stay there long.
By NAMISD.1.4c

Things you learned

What have been the most helpful things that a healthcare professional has said or done for you as they treated this condition?

My first psychiatrist, in a two-hour discussion about whether I would take Prozac, finally said "What have you to lose?" He also told me repeatedly not to talk endlessly about all the details of my bout with depression with my family when I saw them, but just enjoy them for who they are. And that I could always talk about my depression when I came back to the clinic the next day. My therapist in a Christian inpatient clinic, after I had detailed how horrible I thought I was, said "God has forgiven you, can you forgive yourself?"

My California psychiatrist, when I came back home after being in an inpatient clinic and staying with my parents for a time, always reminded me every time I thought about going off my medication, "Remember how horrible the consequences of yours were, and how long it takes you to feel better again. Do you want to take that risk?"
By NAMISD.1.4i

"You are not alone" Together we can find the best treatment possible and with your help and willingness to learn and use your coping skills, you can lead a productive happy life.
By NAMISD.1.4c

What has been the biggest challenge that you've faced in treatment and how have you dealt with it?

I have had great difficulty finding a good, caring, knowledgeable psychiatrist to work with who would be covered by my medical insurance. There is limited access to quality psychiatrists who are not overworked. There are also very few psychiatrists in my area willing to accept Medi-cal/Medicare insurance, and this is the only insurance I have available. I have found it difficult to find psychiatrists I respect, trust, and can have confidence in. Perhaps the greatest difficulty comes in finding a provider who exhibits empathy and compassion within a professional arena of providing knowledgeable feedback and recommendations.
By Anonymous

What have you found to be the best way to successfully communicate and work with healthcare professionals?

Journal, educate myself and have a list of questions. Tell them I want to be a partner in my health care treatment.
By NAMISD.1.4c

What are your impressions of the mental health system? What's good, what's bad, what needs to change?

What has been good and helpful for me has been the Tri-City Outpatient Treatment Program. The continuity of their support has literally kept me alive over the course of the last 10 years with groups in symptoms management, Dialectical Behavior Therapy, STEPS, Dual Recovery, and much more. They have not only been there physically, they have consistently been mentally and emotionally present and available when I needed them. Day by day, week by week I have been supported and encouraged and treated with caring and compassion on a consistent basis. These people are dependable, helpful, kind and loyal. They are accommodating of my needs and frailties. What they have taught me about cognitive therapy, Dialectical Therapy, has been critical to my long term improvement. Their day to day presence in my life has been critical to me. They have been my companions along my life path. It is not an overstatement to say that they are the key to my survival and outcome. I have found that the most basic human capacity for compassion and unconditional support has played a large role in my recovery as the tools of modern medicine.

What has been bad in the mental health system is the length of time required to diagnose my condition and the frequent changes in that diagnosis thereafter. It feels as if the process of diagnosing mental illness is much more a subjective personal decision by an individual physician than an objective evaluation based on scientific knowledge. I have regularly dealt with differing opinions regarding treatment strategies by doctors and outpatient programs, and have found it difficult to locate good psychiatrists and secure adequate medical coverage both for providers and for my medications. This has caused confusion and delays in getting the right medications prescribed. The result has been anxiety and frustration as I often had to stop taking the old meds for 6-8 weeks to get them out of my system before I could start taking the new meds. During the period of time when I would go off the old medications I would sink into deep depressions further aggravating my problem. After finally being able to start the new medications I would then have to wait for them to start working.

The last issue I would mention is that it is extremely difficult to find housing assistance for the homeless who are mentally ill. It took 10 years for me to qualify for HUD housing assistance.

In terms of what needs to change, it is the stigma attached to mental illness by our society. Our culture treats mental health like a moral failing instead of a physical illness.

By Anonymous

My experience tells me our society prefers to take the ostrich approach when it comes to those with mental illness. As a result, there are minimum checks and balances to secure the safety and proper care of those in the system and many, especially in the hospitals and rehab homes that take advantage of the system to the point of neglect and abuse of those with mental illness.

I was shocked, for example, to learn my son was physically being restrained by being tied down on a bed and ultimately died as a result in one of our HOSPITALS.. this is not an isolated incident... This needs to be changed. I understand other states have SUCCESSFULLY stopped using restraints... California can as well. Hospitals and the care system need to be willing to come out of the 18th century and, at least, make an effort to train those who work closely with mental illness not to drug them up and let them sit in a stupor in the corner but to treat them in a calm and compassionate manner. The MENTAL heathcare system needs to pull its head out. They may be surprised at what they find if they think.

By drive1

When Treatment Is Torture: A Personal Account of Seclusion and Restraints

Well, it has been observed by psychologists that the survivors of traumatic events are divided in two well-defined groups: those who repress their past en bloc, and those whose memory of the offense persists, as though carved in stone, prevailing over all previous or subsequent experiences. Now, not by choice but by nature, I belong to the second group.

Primo Levi: Moments of Reprieve: A Memoir of Auschwitz Altogether, I have spent two years of my life in psychiatric hospitals. Some of the staples of institutional living include the following: the strict smoking schedule, anxiously-awaited visiting hours, "Group," the inability to wear shoes, crude art therapy projects, and of course, doctors, nurses and patients who became your allies, friends, or otherwise.

I have to say that I have had weird and occasionally wonderful times at the host of hospitals where I was cared for, but I have experienced the underbelly of the psychiatric treatment protocol as well. As one with bipolar disorder, not only have I been at the mercy of the mental illness itself, but also at the mercy of something equally horrifying and dangerous: seclusion rooms and restraints, used in conjunction with powerful medication. Together, this combination has compounded the trauma of having a mind prone to unraveling on its own.

Of the three times in four-point restraints and seclusion and three times in seclusion alone, I define one incident as torture. This incident made an indelible mark on me and undermined my trust in the process of treatment for many years. This occurred the first time I was admitted to a psychiatric hospital, on my nineteenth birthday, when I was first diagnosed with a mental illness.

November 28th, 1990. I had just finished my Latin final at UCSD. It was the end of the fall quarter of my sophomore year, and I was living on campus. I was supposed to be preparing to go camping. Instead, I was writing passionately in my journal while singing with gusto and energy. I poured a cup of coffee in the fish tank so our pet would experience the ecstasy of elevated consciousness with me. My joy at my cleverness was immense; the fish later died.

When my friend came over to pick me up for our camping trip, not only was I not ready, but I was fragmenting before his eyes. My conversation was unintelligible. I thrust my journal into his hands, my elegant penmanship giving way to a deranged scrawl. I could not stop talking; English turned to gibberish. My mind was dissolving, and fast, my elation and euphoria wiping away my ability to reason.

I was in the midst of manic psychosis. Now, the psychosis was the finale to a series of bizarre and uncharacteristic behaviors, increasing in intensity over a period of months which bewildered and confused my friends. The simple explanation was that "I was going through some stuff" as a result of my father's suicide six months prior.

The chain of events that led to my hospitalization unfolded quickly. The roommates were summoned; the Resident Advisor was summoned; the Resident Dean was summoned. Suddenly, my brother, living at SDSU, appeared from nowhere, yelling at my roommate to find out "what I had taken." My mother and a friend arrived from Los Angeles. I couldn't put the pieces together. Soon, the campus security guard, who I knew and trusted, forced me into my mother's car.

I don't remember being checked into the hospital. I only remember being strapped down. I gaped in horror as the needle of the syringe was inserted into my vein. I screamed. I screamed harder as I watched my brother turn and walk away. The drug started to act, turning my mind of mercury to concrete.

After I was thoroughly drugged, "they" let me lay down on a white bed in a sterile room with my hospital clothes on. When I woke up, I didn't know where I was or why. There was a plate of plastic-looking food which I promptly threw in the trash. I walked onto the unit and saw a whiteboard with lines and words I couldn't read. A nurse soon plied me with a plastic shot glass of "orange juice," which I swallowed. My lips puckered, and I determined she was lying: it couldn't be real orange juice.

The door of a storage closet was open. Inside were shelves upon shelves of crates and cartons filled with art supplies. I couldn't make out the closet's contents completely, but I was motivated. The only thing obstructing my complete view was a large male nurse in scrubs who stood in front of the open doorway. I tried running into the storage room door, but instead, ran into the nurse.

My next memory was finding myself in four-point restraints, strapped to a metal table, naked, in a seclusion room with dark brown walls and the incessant hum of an industrial-sized air conditioner. On the wall, there was an intercom which at first I assumed was a working intercom, but no one responded to my questions. Eventually my tongue swelled up and would hardly move. I could not say my name, although I tried many times. Lastly, there was a dot of red light above my head, which I presumed to be part of a surveillance camera. I became convinced "they" wanted to kill me as part of a research project.

My memory is fragmented, but I know I was there for three days. I sat in a pool of urine for many hours. I saw no familiar faces, only a nurse with garish make-up and her two "henchmen." They would come in periodically, leave a plate of food on the floor, untie me long enough to try and eat and defecate in a kidney-shaped plastic bed pan, and come back and tie me back up. The woman only observed as the men "worked."

On one occasion, my innate sense of rebellion flared, and I decided to get out of the restraints by any means necessary. Fox-like, I started to lubricate my right wrist with saliva, and after toiling for many hours, I slipped my hand out of the restraint. I relished the small victory. Soon after, the scary nurse appeared with her henchmen again, and she laughed. "It looks like we've got a little escape artist on our hands." The male nurses corrected the situation and tightened all of my restraints, especially the right hand I had set free.

Eventually I was transferred out of that hospital by ambulance and back to a hospital in my hometown, Northridge, in the San Fernando Valley, to be close to my mother. I was discharged after only a week and soon returned to UCSD for the winter quarter, lithium in hand, but otherwise with no acknowledgement that anything had happened.

This was my first exposure to mental health care, before I had heard the word "bipolar." I was new to the system, but I had the bruises on my wrists and ankles to prove that I was a now full-fledged member of this sometimes counter-productive world of medicine.

Later in life, my mind has been caught in psychosis, where thoughts of this experience engulf me, submerging sanity. It was in that hospital that I acquired those specific memories that once seared on the mind will not die until I do, classic scars of trauma. For that, the psychiatric practice of using seclusion and restraints to control already sick people should be condemned.
By NAMISD.1.6h

Parenting a Child with Mental Illness

Things that happened

What initially made you think your child might have a mental illness and when did this happen?

Our child was a very angry teenager and mean to their siblings.
By Anonymous

Unfortunately, mental illness is the Sword of Damocles in our family. Both my husband and I have first degree relatives with either Schizophrenia or Paranoid Bipolar disease. I was always worried about any child of ours being born with Schizophrenia BUT I never worried about Bipolar Disorder...denial that my genes could cause any harm to our son. Our first child came out of the womb different, chronically irritable, chronically dissatisified, unable to adapt to flexible schedules, always different....

I was due to deliver our second child and was extremely concerned about the aggression our 3 year-old displayed whenever he didn't get what he wanted. I took him to a local child psychiatrist who stated that he thought he was just fine. Then our second child was born and the aggression was worse. We went to a child psychologist who "worked" with him for three years and then said she could "do no more, that he was going to grow up into a fine young man." Our family lived through hellish years while waiting for that day to occur. So, when did I think he was mentally ill.   LONG BEFORE THE PROFESSIONALS!

By Anonymous

My son's condition showed up when he was in pre-school about the age of three, three and a half. Brent was not socializing and not getting along with the other kids in his class. He became quite irritable. His teacher didn't use the words mental illness but said he was exhibiting adjustment issues. She suggested that I hold him back a year to give him one more year to mature before entering kindergarten. Unfortunately, because of my divorce, my own illness and my need to work I couldn't to have him out of school. I needed him to be in school so I could be in bed. I needed three uninterrupted hours in bed where I didn't feel the need to get up and take care of the needs of small children. I was desperate for that time alone just so I could function. I felt I had no choice other than to let Brent go into kindergarten. I had assumed that if he didn't progress, that I could just hold him back at the end of kindergarten and he could repeat it the next year. What I didn't realize at that time is that they would not let him repeat kindergarten. They pushed him ahead into first grade even though he wasn't ready for it emotionally. His condition became worse as the pressures of school mounted. Brent became increasingly sensitive, irritable, moody and depressed. He was formally diagnosed in 1988 at age 7.

As Brent grew we struggled to provide adequate medical treatment for his condition. As my ex-husband changed jobs his insurance refused to cover our son's illness claiming it was a pre-existing medical condition. In spite of his illness Brent's dream was to be in show business, and he had a certain amount of success. He was in a Steve Martin movie, "L.A. Story," sharing his own scene with one other actor. He also got involved in plays. He starred as Oliver in 81 performances at the Lawrence Welk Resort. He did commercials and print jobs, and magazines. We were constantly on the way up to Hollywood for auditions. He also had problems in school. He had learning disabilities, and even though he was very

73

bright with an IQ tested over 140 he had trouble maintaining a B average – which was required by SAG for him to work in the entertainment industry. Unfortunately, I was so ill that I didn't have the time to help him with his school work which only made the situation worse.

When he was 13 things tragically changed. Brent had spent the day rehearsing for a job in Las Vegas, and had another performance at a café in the area singing with a band. When he came home that evening, much to my annoyance Brent had brought home with him the son of the youth pastor. This meant that I had to take this boy home and I was mad at my son for putting me in that position. I was off all of my medications at the time because I was transitioning to another prescription so I was also depressed, stressed, irritable and testy. I had not planned on this additional task this evening. I did not want to deal with chauffeuring another teenager. I was more abrupt and cross with my son than I normally would have been. I was not in a good place and Brent was a very sensitive. He was hurt and angry at me when I left. The biggest mistake I made was not leaving a friend of his there with him when I left to drive the other boy home. Brent was alone at a time when he should not have been, but I did not realize that at the time.

When I came home I found Brent had hung himself from a rope in the back yard. I cut him down from the rope and tried to do CPR. The little girl he had been rehearsing with (who was his best friend) called 911. It took about 10 minutes for help to arrive, but by then it was too late. They pronounced him dead on the scene. I went into the hospital that night.
By Anonymous

How did you come to get a diagnosis for your child? What is that diagnosis?

Any parent with a child with mental illness ultimately learns they will have multiple diagnoses before they're presented with one that seems to fit. It appears that many children are initially diagnosed with ADHD. Of course, when they have an adverse reaction to the medication...like, it triggers a manic episode, we learn that the diagnosis is incorrect.

I kept telling the multiple child psychiatrists that I believed our son had Bipolar Disorder but they kept saying that they "couldn't diagnose mental illness in young children." Of course, we know that is incorrect. Our first "real" diagnosis occurred when our son had his first breakdown at 11 years old and was hospitalized in a child-adolescent mental health unit. THEN, the inpatient psychiatrist decided that he had not only Bipolar Disorder, but Conduct Disorder, ODD, and ADHD.

So, it took 8 years from the time I had taken him to his first mental health professional at 3 years old until he was 11 years old for a working diagnosis to be given to us. The diagnosis at this time is Atypical Bipolar Disorder...a catch all for crossover symptoms that also appear Schizophrenic but not that diagnosis.
By Anonymous

My daughter's first psychiatrist gave her a diagnosis of schizo/affective disorder and that diagnosis is still the same today with the exception of periods when she changed doctors and noncompliant with her meds.
By jasmine69

What have been the barriers and successes in working with healthcare professionals to help your child?

The biggest barriers are the unwillingness to diagnose children when they are young, for fear of "stigmatizing" them, professionals who don't refer to others when a child's behavior is beyond their scope of practice and or experience, professionals who are not aware of resources in the community to refer families to for further help, professionals who prefer to think that it is inadequate parenting skills, neurotic mother syndrome, that they know more and don't listen, and professionals who keep you returning without really helping because you're a "cash cow" for them especially when you are not using insurance and can pay their full fee.

In the 19 years that I've been dealing with the professionals who have "taken care" of my child, only two really listened to my concerns and tried to work with our child and our family. Most were insufferably arrogant and felt they knew better.
By Anonymous

What have been your experiences with institutions – like child care providers, school systems, or your work – that involve your child's illness?

SCHOOL SYSTEMS...what a horrible joke! I tried to get an IEP for my son when he was entering sixth grade. He was suffering from depression and I wanted the teachers to know what had caused it, what to look for, how to contact me, etc... Because of the process, he had the testing and the IEP meeting and was then denied any services because he didn't need "extra help." Not only was he denied help, the school psychologist had the audacity to write in her assessment that "the parents should seek counseling to determine why he has so much anger." NEVER, did this "professional" ask what we had already done to "determine why he had so much anger."

He had his first Bipolar break that year, four months after they denied that he had any problems. He was hospitalized and only then did the IEP team reconsider and determine that he was eligible for Special Education and put him in a class with Severely Emotionally Disturbed students. That was a horrible mistake, because he was further exposed to outrageous behaviors which either incited him to act out more or scared him. After his second Bipolar hospitalization, the vice-principal decided they didn't want him at the school any longer, that he was a danger to himself and others, and the IEP team recommended a school for students that were severely emotionally disturbed.

We declined their offer and made our own plans for our son. Since we decided what we wanted to do without consulting the IEP team or the AB2726 workers, we were then denied public mental health care. I have found with the school system that you are dammed if you do and dammed if you don't. It's really a miserable institution to work with, has uninformed personnel making decisions based on their fears and biases, rather than logical, scientific information.
By Anonymous

What have you experienced with this child that has changed your relationships with your other children and family members?

My family thought that I was "making a mountain out of a molehill." True words spoken by my mother who was in her own denial that mental illness had passed through the family genes. For years, that colored any interactions that we had with her. My sister thought he'd be better with her family since we "couldn't handle him." Well, they both would have been extremely sorry had I had him live with them. The destruction of property, the "walking on eggshells," the blow-ups, stealing, lying, and manipulating would have changed their minds in a hurry but ultimately would have been much more detrimental to his well-being.

I always tried to make time for my younger child so that he won't feel like he was being shunted aside, this was done through soccer. He started playing when he was six and I attended all practices, games, went to tournaments with him, was team mom, you name it...just so he could feel that he had a place in our family that wasn't "contaminated" by his brothers behavior. However, even that wasn't enough...as he entered his teens, he began experiencing the side effects of the trauma that our family lived through and has been coping with finding out who he is, why isn't he what he remembered being when he was younger?

It's difficult seeing the havoc that mental illness causes in families. However, there is another side to this. I have found that living with and helping my children cope with mental illness has transformed me. I'm more willing to give children and people displaying unusual behaviors the benefit of the doubt instead of just assuming they're "bad kids or junkies on the street." I discovered a patience, an empathy, and a genuine concern for the betterment of the lives of people with mental illness. I believe this has affected my children, in that I'm not willing to judge them as quickly, they know I'm there to support them, and above all...they know they are LOVED unconditionally!
By Anonymous

I have only one child, but I wanted him to know how much I love him. I always tell him, you're my number one son and he says I am your only son, and I say see, I tell the truth! He has taught me lots of patience and he has taught me to really accept people as they are. I feel as though he is special, not to say he doesn't make things difficult at times but I have learned to be more creative. I have used the things he taught me to help me deal with my family in better ways. I think of how he trusts me and how he tells me about his world. I think that is good, because when I grew up, I hid things like my thoughts a lot because I had been made fun of by the other kids at my school. My son can tell me anything and he knows I will understand him. I am not saying that I don't get tired of hearing it all the time, but we talk and I listen to him. I have learned to ask him questions that help him think too. I take what I learn from him and help others and I learn from others and use what I learn from others to help me. He has helped me to see how much my mom loves me because he has given me the chance to be a good mommy to him. I am thankful for that.

By Anonymous

How has your child's condition impacted the way you parent?

I must say, I didn't know what parenting meant other than loving, supporting, feeding, caring, and helping. I didn't know that you were supposed to LISTEN to what your child had to say because my family didn't listen. We were told what to do, think, feel. That was a definite weakness that was initially introduced to my children but because of our older child's mental illness was a weakness that had to change rather quickly.

I read every book on the market regarding parenting when our son was still a baby. NONE of them fit this child. It made me so frustrated that I couldn't find an algorithm to help me rear him because I was so unprepared. Ultimately, I started trusting my instincts...defying my husband's desire for stricter discipline, disregarding my family telling me I was "spoiling" my children because I was "giving in" too often. But, I won't change how I ultimately ended up parenting my children. It was hard, it was a long time of miscommunication, balancing being too permissive and too authoritarian, to finally achieve the place where they knew they could be listened to without being judged, not told what to do, what to think, when to do it, when to stop.

79

You know, we are allowed to become parents without knowing much about parenting. We can't drive a car or become licensed professionals, without learning what to do FIRST. Once we've shown competency then we are allowed to proceed. Those of us who weren't raised in "NORMAL" families (if indeed there really is such a thing) don't know that we are setting dangerous practices loose in our own families and don't know there are better ways UNTIL things are out of hand and we have to seek help. What a sorry situation our society is in by not training people to become parents BEFORE they are in that situation.

How has my child's condition impacted the way I parent? EVERY way you can think.
By Anonymous

What impact has your child's condition had on your marriage?

To be honest, I don't know how we've managed to stay together. Neither of us came from families where the marriages were sound, stable, happy, healthy. Our marriage has weathered anger, disgust, hurt feelings, frustration, apathy, feelings of betrayal because we didn't feel like our individual attitudes of parenting were respected by the other, long silences, and maybe finally the realization that neither one of us were completely correct and our spouse wasn't completely incorrect about everything they did or say.

Raising a child with mental illness either pulls you together or pushes you apart. I think sheer stubbornness or perhaps exhaustion has kept us together. We don't give up easily and the thought of abandoning our responsibilities to our children and ourselves isn't in the picture. I am so thankful that we have managed to stay together because it's time to reap the rewards of this long fight and look forward to children who are healthy enough

to function. Perhaps, not in the way we wanted for them when they were babies, but in the way that's healthiest for them.
By Anonymous

Our adult son, our only child, was diagnosed with bipolar disorder in 2004. He lived out of state and was 25, living and working on his own. We stayed in close contact with him but were not "on site" to monitor his meds, his therapy, etc. He was on his own and working hard to recover after his psychotic break that landed him in the Psychiatric ward. Eleven months after his diagnosis, Todd couldn't stand the racing thoughts and voices (yes, Bipolar has them, too), and he took his life. We were shocked, totally numb with the surreal nature of this sudden and tragic "new normal." But instead of driving my husband and I apart, it drove us into each other's arms and into each other's grief. We absolutely do not have a perfect marriage, but we have a very secure and committed one. That was a lifesaver! Our grief styles were totally opposite: He sobbed and I worked. We soon learned that grief is unique and solitary and we had to honor each other's grieving. The difference was so stark that if we had not made this decision, we would have drifted apart and resented each other. Because we chose to walk together through the grief, even if the style was "together—alone", we have been able to work alongside others who have experienced similar losses. While we miss our son with every breath we take, we are grateful for the bond that did NOT break.
By CK

We divorced in 1986 about two years before Brent's formal diagnosis. The health insurance companies that my ex-husband had through work would not pay for the "pre-existing condition" of my son's depression, and my ex-husband had refused to pay for out of pocket expenditures for doctors and/or treatment. This created enormous tension, resentment and depression on my part.

My ex-husband was also an alcoholic and this added to the demise of the marriage.

I became bitter and angry and my own mental illness became worse. As I delved deeper into depression, both children started living with their alcoholic father who was also abusive and angry. The children's lives were difficult as they struggled to make sense of their worlds. I'm sure this all contributed to my son's depression. After my son committed suicide my ex-husband's drinking became worse. Although we maintained a relationship even after our divorce, and he lived in the apartment right behind me, my ex-husband died alone and in great emotional pain.

By Anonymous

How has your child's condition changed the way you see yourself?

I always knew I was a strong woman. But boy did I find out just how strong I was while dealing with my child's mental illness. I took on my family, my husband, the schools, the mental health professionals, and didn't stop until I got the best treatment for my child. I changed from a self-centered young woman to one who developed an enormous reservoir of empathy for people in the same condition as my son. I became a mental health advocate, started speaking about our experiences to anyone who would listen and was SHOCKED at the number of people who responded that they also had someone who "was different" in their family.

I have been teaching NAMI Family to Family classes for 8 years, I have become a California State Trainer to teach other people interested in teaching families about mental illness for both adults and for children through their NAMI BASICS education program. I talk to teachers, school nurses, anybody that I can to educate them about mental illness in our children and adolescents. I have become a genuinely caring person due to my child's condition. I don't know that I would have become as introspective or deep a person without this experience.

I once told my son that I was so happy that he was my child because through him I learned to have patience and compassion. He got a big smile on his face, put his arms around me, and told me that he was so happy that I told him that.
By Anonymous

Because of my mental illness, I was living only in the present, trying to make it through one day at a time. I had no future and I couldn't see the future for my children. I was too ill to see or think about anything other than what was immediately in front of me.
By Anonymous

What or who are the most important resources and advocates that you have found or still need to find?

One word....NAMI! The National Alliance on Mental Illness.

Thank heaven I found this organization. I was lost, didn't know who to talk to, didn't know anybody who had been through the same experiences I had, could find no information that was helpful or if I found it it was so scary that I couldn't read it. One day I heard about this organization. I called...and hung up, too afraid to talk to the person at the other end of the line, too afraid to say out loud what had happened to my family, to my beloved child. I called twice more and again hung up before I found the courage to stay on the line and get help.

What I got was compassion, understanding, someone who could listen to me as I was crying on the phone. What I got was immeasurable. Resources, information, educational classes about mental illness, being with other families who had been or currently were in the same situation I found myself. What I got was a sanity saver.

More people need to know about NAMI. More people need to discover what this organization can do to help them in times of need.

PEOPLE....call your local NAMI for help, log on to the national website. You'll never be sorry!
By Anonymous

Is there anything else that has happened to you or that you've experienced in this area that you would like to share?

Parents...trust your instincts! Don't let "professionals" cow you, don't feel that since they are "professionals" and know more than you, they don't know YOUR child as well as you do.

Don't be afraid to say NO to things you don't agree with but don't say NO just to be assertive. Judge what you hear and read with a logical and scientific process. READ, be up to date on terminology, study about the medications and their side effects, don't be afraid to question anybody...schools, mental health professionals, or anyone else who feels they know more than you. Honestly, they only know what they've been taught and it isn't a "one size fits all" type of approach.

Don't allow yourself to fall into the stigma of mental health and be ashamed to talk about it to people. Enlighten them when they think you are a bad parent, you'd be surprised at how many have this in their homes but are in denial and therefore are not helping their children because they can't admit there is something wrong.

Remember you can lead a horse to water but you can't make it drink. Well, you can lead families to insight but don't feel you are a failure if they don't listen to your advice based on experience and knowlege. Don't be afraid to talk about mental illness...it's one of our most potent weapons against stigma.

By Anonymous

My husband had died of suicide in the spring of 1990. Three months later my daughter was diagnosed with bi-polar illness. She had had a total breakdown in the fall of her sophmore year in college. She was hospitalized and received professional care from good psychiatrists. After her recovery, she seemed to adjust to her college environment, was on medication, and was getting good grades.

The following year my daughter was selected to attend her junior year abroad. I was very excited and yet worried about her. She had been taking medication and was under a doctor's care. She had assured me that she had been taking her medication on a regular basis. She stated that she was "ready" and capable of traveling "across the pond" to attend college in England. The problem was that she wasn't getting her paper work ready for the application process and couldn't find it. Being a very organized and helpful parent, I was determined to help her find it and get the paper work complete. I found it and she finally completed the information! She went to England in the fall of 1992.

In retrospect, I would not have helped her in any way. I didn't realize that even though she was bright, if she couldn't find the paper work and didn't want to rummage through her college files, she probably was fearful about the trip. The result was a total mental breakdown in a foreign country. Her academic work was excellent, but she had stopped taken her medication and was hospitalized for five long months! She was hospitalized from November 1991 to March of 1992. England at that time, did not believe in the use of Lithium for bi-polar patients. I traveled to England, made numerous phone calls, talked to her seemingly competent doctor, but they refused to give her the recommended medications prescribed in this county. Her doctor stated to me that in time her manic stage would pass, she would come down to a depressive state, and then she would be released to come home. I decided then, that I would not take charge of a matter that would force her into a situation that she was not capable of handling.

By Anonymous

Things you learned

What do you wish you had done or not done in getting to a diagnosis and seeking help for your child?

I wish I had been more knowlegable about my family's mental illness BEFORE I had children.

I wish I had known about the concordance rate of passing this illness along to those innocent babies before I had them.

I wish I had not been so naive about what it meant to be a parent, the battle of proving to yourself and others, over and over, that my instincts were valid, that rejecting other's advice was many times in the best interest of my child and I wish they would have accepted that without fighting me about everything.

I wish there had been a facility in my city where I could have sent my son for help instead of sending him away for treatment. I wish I had known about the public mental health system and how it worked before we had to take 2nd and 3rd mortgages to pay for his various treatments.

I wish I had been more prepared.
By Anonymous

How have you most successfully communicated on behalf of your child with schools, childcare providers or other outsiders?

Once when my child was small, he and another child went into the bathroom with scissors and the other boy asked mine to cut his hair so mine did. When I went to pick him up that day, one of the teachers was kinda giving me a hard time. I asked her about two girls sitting down at a table and said,"if it were those two girls would you be this upset?" She said "no, of course not, they're normal" and I said, "do you realize what you just said?" She realized what I was implying and immediatly apologized to me. She didn't realize how or what she was saying that I thought was unfair. I knew she wasnt trying to be mean or anything. So then we talked about how the mentally ill are sometimes treated unfairly because they are sometimes labled trouble makers. This lady was really nice and I knew she hadn't tried to hurt me or my son. After that she always asked my advice on how to talk to other parents about their kids so she wouldnt make a mistake or pick on other mentally ill kids or their parents! You know what? She really wanted to be aware of what we go through and I had many wonderful conversations with her the rest of the year and after that too. I wonder how she is doing these days, but I do know she really cared and she really wanted to treat everyone well.

I have found that many people in the field of care are ignorant to our needs and sometimes they don't think about things until we point it out or take the time to educate them. Some of them are only wanting to hear only good things and they really lack empathy. I really feel some people shouldnt be in the field. I do have one funny story though, I was at work one day. One of my co-workers asked me how I could understand the mentally ill so well, so I told her I was mentally ill too. She asked me how I got to work and I said very casually, in my car. She asked me who drove me to work and I said I drive myself. She asked me (in a serious way) they let you drive? I said, yes, I don't use meds to make me nutty, I take them for thinking and to help me have better days, of course I can drive. What makes you think we can't drive? It was sorta funny because she really didn't know and we both laughed. I told her in a joking way, the only time I am not able to drive is after midnight when I turn into a tree! She now has a completely different outlook and is a very kind and caring person. She just didn't know. I think sometimes people don't try to make mean remarks they just sorta think we don't know how to do some things.

Be patient and "teach" a care provider some great things about yourself, then you can change how they see us. I try to keep my heart and my mind open. I love to talk with people, in fact the ones I like the most are those who have problems because we all have problems and I can help destroy the myths about mental illness. I really like to surprise people and they learn about me too. I always try to be respectful and honest with whomever I speak with.
By NAMISD.1.5a

How do you deal with the stress that a child with mental illness places on a marriage?

We take turns supporting each other, when one of us is down or overloaded, the other steps in to interact with our child and /or support the one who has taken most of the interaction with the child.

By Anonymous

Are there any other things that you have learned about this topic that you would like to share with us? What are we not asking you, that we should be asking you, if we knew to ask it?

This is a look back. I wish I had understood a very important rule with males: ONE question or request at a time! I just did not learn that until later. Males do not multitask like females and it really creates havoc with their minds.

If I knew this, I would never had expected my son to multitask. I would not have been upset when he could not do "this and then that, and then that."

If I had known this, I would have known to talk less. I have learned men can't handle the constant speaking of woman.

I wish I had taken off from work - actually a leave of absence may have been best to be able to be home. I managed too many tasks - not good.

I just didn't have anywhere to turn to get answers I could understand. I did not know what mental illness was and even now still have some problems.

When his last doctor did not get back to me, I wish I had known where he was and had driven down to find him, meet him (this never happened until after our son's funeral), and talk to him about my knowledge about my son.

When my instincts told me things were not right, I wish I would have known to fight back --- to be HEARD!

I would like to stand up for moms! We know our babies - age does not matter.

I would also like to tell others if you hear the word restrain used, it does not mean help or hold, it means "tie up" (and for our son it also meant ignore til death).
By BC

When our son Todd was diagnosed with bipolar disorder he was in his mid-twenties and lived 1,000 miles from home. His dad and I were abruptly thrust into an unknown and uninvited universe—the world of mental illness. Then came the flurry of uncomfortable emotions, frightening premonitions, free-floating fears. We felt helpless and uninformed. What is Bipolar? How serious is this? What causes it? What cures it? Can the doctors fix it? Can WE?

We shuddered as we considered what might be ahead for us as a family. There were ugly whispers of guilt and shame; we couldn't nail them down to specifics. Instead, they just hovered in the air above us like unspoken blame. We should have parented better; we should have paid more attention to Todd; we should have watched for warning signs; we should have allowed him to make more of his own decisions; we should have given him a sibling so he wouldn't have felt so alone. We should have. These were our "sins of omission"—things left undone.

And then the mental hammer came down on the overt parenting failures that might have set Todd up for this fall: The arguments and disagreements. Too much duty, not enough fun. The stress and strain of our work that too often took precedence over Todd's needs and wants. And the words—too many and often too sharp. These were indictments that cut to the heart.

When parents deal with mental illness in their own children it is a given that they assume some level of responsibility and remorse. After all, Todd was a combination of Rex and my DNA; he had no say there. Nor did he have a voice to accept or reject the experiences, environments, geographies or beliefs that shaped him. So what could we have done differently, done better, done more of, stopped doing, that might have equipped Todd to deal with this?

As I have wrestled with the "shoulds" and the "shouldn't haves", I have arrived at a conclusion that I can live with: WE DID THE BEST WE COULD. Our "best" did not cure Todd; bipolar took his life a year after he was diagnosed. But the best thing we could do for Todd was to love him well and love him unconditionally. As parents that is what we should have done. In the end, that is what we did, holding nothing back. This was our very best.
By CK

Encountering the
Legal System

Things that happened

Why, when and where have you had to deal with the legal or criminal justice system as a result of a mental illness?

In retrospect my son was ill for two years but we did not know what was going on. One night after we went to bed he was doing some "work" in our garage as he often did after we went to bed so he would not have to encounter or interact with any family members. We awoke to a terrible sound outside. My son had assaulted a neighbor in order to protect our family from some delusional impending attack. Our neighbor died from his wounds. Our son was arrested and prosecuted for murder. We were removed from our home that night and taken the police station. For emotional reasons we were never able to return to the home we were raising our four children in. My son spent 2 years in jail and after 30 day trial he was found "not guilty by reason of insanity." He is currently receiving treatment in a state hospital.
By Anonymous

Two unimaginable realities came to light for me in the past 10 years. One, I would never have imagined that MY adult son would ever have an encounter with the criminal justice system. Two, I never expected that having a mental illness (a biological brain disorder) would result in my son doing more time in jail and prison than he ever has in a psychiatric hospital, since his first psychotic break 10 years ago to the present.

There are no men in the "white coats" that I used to see on T.V. , who would come to the home and take the person to the hospital where family could visit, give loving support and comfort, and let their loved one know that this was the best and they would be okay. Instead, I would be told "he is not a danger to himself or others" and shortly after the paronia and other psychotic symptoms of his illness would lead him to the streets, ultimately finding street drugs and alcohol to self medicate, become one of the homeless, and ultimately get arrested.

My NAMI San Diego resources advised me to frequently check the "who's in jail" link on the Sheriffs website so that upon his arrest, I could get to his court hearing to advocate for mental health treatment and not punishment and incarceration for my son. This only made common sense that they would read the arrest reports, SEE the obvious symptoms of his psychosis displayed during the court hearing, and take in to account his previous 21 year history of "normalcy" that I (his mother) presented to the court. By the way, I need to explain that none of my son's arrests involved violence, harm to another person or theft. I always say all his crimes were against himself, and that even these crimes were due to "lack of insight" a major symptom of his diagnosis.
By Anonymous

My family and I have had to deal with the legal system at different times. When my brother is off his medication and refuses treatment we have to call the police and have them get involved to force my brother to get help. My brother is not only a schizophrenic but also happens to have diabetes. He takes insulin in the morning & then a different one at night, the injection shots may vary. Therefore, sometimes I have had to call the paramedics and the police to make sure my brother gets treatment for his own well being.

Other times have been that my brother threatened someone and that person filed charges and my brother I

93

believe went to jail for about 1 year or so. I thought that was pretty stupid because he is mentally ill. I have mixed feelings about the whole legal system. I find that some people help and others don't seem to care. Some agencies like the police that I have encountered since my brother got home from the Army, the Police have all been nice and humane and treated me and my family with respect & dignity. Not sure if its because my brother went to serve his country & came back with a mental illness. Then on the other hand, I get upset at the judges & attorneys who take on these cases but do not contact the family for whatever reason to have them explain or provide information that pertains to a sibling with mental illness. Court hearings are sometimes done behind close doors and family members are not always allowed, at least that has been my experience.

By grome_420

Was there any build up to your encounter with the legal system or did the situation come out of nowhere?

My son had never had any encounters with the legal system until his illness. His illness became progressively worse over about one year after he graduated from H.S. and there was one incident that resulted in a 5150. After that he was put on a very low dose of an atypical. Over the next year he seemed to be okay, not good but not as bad as before the 5150. About 3 days before his crime he started to exhibit subtle behaviors that concerned my daughter but nothing that would have given any insight into what he would do. The signs were an indication that he was falling into a dark place however. This violent crime was totally out of character and something unimaginable to us. It still is after 8 years.

By Anonymous

Who did you turn to for legal help and how did you find them?

This crime is as severe as it gets. We turned to a private attorney but ultimately used a public defender. His defense would have been unaffordable otherwise. I must say that the public defender's office did a wonderful job not only because of the outcome but because of all of the fact gathering, investigative work and expert testimony that was used for an appropriate defense.
By Anonymous

How long did it take to work your way through the legal process and what were the costs?

It took 2 years to go to trial. There were many steps along the way. Receiving psychological and psychiatric opinions were very time consuming. The costs were were quite substantial I'm sure. This would not be affordable for most with private legal help.
By Anonymous

What was the outcome? Is the situation resolved or is it on-going?

After a 30 day trial my son was found not guilty by reason of insanity and was sentenced to a state hospital.
By Anonymous

What impact did your encounter with the legal system have on you and those close to you?

The legal system was foreign to us but this situation gave us an education that no one wants. I know that justice was served because the evidence for insanity was overwhelming and the appropriate placement was carried out but in spite of the overwhelming evidence, the prosecution's desired outcome made this process almost too much to bear. I will be permanently jaded by what I witnessed as information was presented to the court in a context that had no resemblance to reality. Thankfully the truth did prevail.

By Anonymous

In the the State of California, San Diego County, the criminal justice system does not bode well for persons living with mental illness... I morphed into an advocate for change in the criminal justice system for not only my son but for all those who have the unfortunate experience of being arrested and have a mental illness and their family/friends. At times when I saw the public defender and court appointed defense attorney "collaborating" before my family member's case was even presented, no consultation with him, or his family (actually they were often shocked that family was present). Jail and Prison is a pretty bad place, I can't even imagine what my son endured with his "active" symptoms present.

By Anonymous

It has been my experience that the attorneys that are appointed to represent the mentally ill clients might not be experts in that field. I feel that to the court appointed attorneys my brother is just another file, another pro bono case to work on. They don't take the time to contact family members or give the family members a chance to speak on behalf of that person, in our case my brother. I don't remember ever having a single attorney contact us to get our perspective of the situation or to speak on behalf of my brother to have the judge hear us so he can get a better understanding that my brother is cared for & loved & has family to speak for him and that my brother is not a loose cannon waiting to go off like they usually lead the public to believe in so many cases that involve a person with a mental illness.

The attorneys need to be more sympathetic and show compassion and talk to family members so that the attorney can better understand the client better and in the end get his client help! Not incarceration. That's not always the solution, and the punishment doesn't always seem to fit the crime.
By grome_420

What or who was your most important resource during this process?

Obviously my son's defense team was the most important resource but it is critical to understand that as family members, we are a part of that team also. The severity of the offense does not matter. An attorney not armed with the history and progression of the illness will not be able to mount the best defense possible. My role throughout the 2 years leading up to the trial was critical to the outcome. I spent hundreds of hours preparing information for the attorneys, investigators and medical experts. I spent scores of hours speaking with all of them with goal that they will know my son as well as I do when I am done. Then they will know the only logical explanation for such a crime is a psychosis so severe it would drive delusions with devastating consequences.
By Anonymous

Things you learned

What have you learned about working with attorneys, the courts, prosecutors, the police,

97

the prison system, probation officers, etc. that you wish you knew beforehand?

I learned that sobriety, med-compliancy, faith in GOD and a good attitude make all the difference in the world.
By NAMISD.1.3d

I don't actually believe some of the treatment my son/we received was done out of malice or unconcern. It was about Stigma, not knowing how to assist a person living with mental illness in the criminal justice system, the type of services needed not being available or not enough to serve the number of people in the criminal justice system, and of course MONEY to provide services.
By Anonymous

That not everyone is willing to help, that not everyone has the best interest of someone with mental illness, but that once in a while you will come across someone who is kind, willing to help and shows compassion for you, your family and your sibling with mental illness.
By Anonymous

What were your impressions of the legal system when it came to dealing with mental illness? What works, what doesn't, what needs to change?

Education, Education, Training, Training, and more Education and Training. I beleive every agency in the criminal justice system should have a mandated NAMI In Our Own Voice presentation designed for this system. Every Parole and Probation department should have a complete list of all services available for their clients who live with mental illness. There should be a transistion plan done 3-6 months before release where person being

98

released is picked up from release location by parole/probation/mental health program representatives and have some type of support (Peer Support would work great in these instances) to help them maneuver through the system.

By Anonymous

Showing compassion for the mentally ill and for their families. Finding solutions other than incarcerations. Hearing family members speak so that judges can make an informative decision, maybe helping families in getting temporary conservatorship for that mentally ill family member. What has worked for us is getting a conservator for my brother and having that conservator have contact with the family to know our concerns and needs as well as for my brothers.

By Anonymous

There are three and each reflects my impression of the way three different police officers treated my brother. When my brother was in early adolescence he developed a nasty combination of OCD / Anxiety Disorder / ADD. This was further aggravated by drug abuse and the divorce of our parents. By the time he was 13 he came to believe that he was smarter than everyone else. By the time he was 16 he was sure of it, and equally positive that everyone else was an idiot. He thought the rules didn't apply to him and that he could outsmart any system or anyone.

He was working in a take-out pizza parlour when either he or one of his friends had the idea to fake a robbery. He was working alone late at night and there were no surveilance cameras at that time. All he had to do was have a friend walk in when the place was empty, ask for (more like pick up) the cash, and leave. Ten minutes after the friend (co-conspirator) left my brother called the police to report an armed robbery. The police arrived, my brother went through his act, gave the police a false description of the robber, and then came home to be consoled by my mother who was now panicked that her son had been robbed.

This act went off so well that my brother and his accomplice bragged to nearly everyone they knew about how smart they were and how they had outsmarted the police. (They made sure not to tell me.) That was their undoing. It turns out that at least a few of the kids they told had a moral compass afterall, and they tipped off the police to the fact that the geniuses were about to do it again at another pizza parlour in the chain. The police hid and waited for the faux holdup to take place. They watched as the first guy went into the pizza parlour and when he demanded the cash acting like a robber they jumped out from behind the counter and nailed him. At the same time the police who were out in the parking lot pounced on my brother who was sitting behind the wheel of a van (aka the getaway car). Here's where my impressions start.

We came to learn a few hours later that the arresting officer yelled "FREEZE." My brother was surprised and apparently jerked his head around to see who was yelling - which is somewhat to be expected. This officer read my brother's actions as a threat and pulled the trigger on his handgun - a 45 caliber with hollow point bullets. The gun misfired. The hammer left an impression in the firing pin of the round, but the round did not go off. Had the gun fired that round would have decapitated my brother and killed him instantly. The officer was reportedly 15 feet away and behind my brother when he yelled. He was certainly close enough to see that he was deciding to shoot and kill a 16-year-old kid.

Impression number one is that even though the officer was in no peril he thought himself to be. My brother was unarmed, but the officer didn't know that and he acted to preserve his own life, not the life of a kid. He didn't know of my brother's illness and he didn't care. Fear often drives the police, and if I had their job I probably would feel the same way.

Impression number two. About 1:30 in the morning the police called my mother to tell her that her son was in jail for armed robbery. I went down to the police station around 2AM to see if we could see my brother. We were turned away at the front desk by the officer in charge who proceeded to explain to my hysterical mother that her son was very lucky because he had almost had his head blown off - a point he repeated several times. The point that bothers me about this man's behavior to this day is that he so clearly enjoyed torturing my mother over this point. The more distraught she became the more he teed off on her. Whether he felt that he was trying to scare her straight into being a better parent, or chastising her for her failures as a mother, I don't know. He didn't know the whole story, and he didn't care, but he was going to extract his pound of flesh from the low-lifes of society and we, for that moment, fit the bill. My second impression is that judgement in the absence of all the facts is misguided, unproductive and often cruel. Sadly, I think I also engage in this kind of behavior way too often.

Third impression. I found out in the coming days after my brother made bail that one of the officers had sat with him all night in his cell talking to him about what he had done. He told my brother that very few parents ever evidence the concern for their child that my mother had. This man tried to reason with and help a deeply troubled kid. I don't know how much of an impact that early morning talk really had on my brother over time, but it had an impact then and it continues to have an impact on me. There are people out there, many in law enforcement who are decent people and care deeply. They try to do the right things and are a credit to their profession. We should never lump all people into the same category or tar all police with one brush. The simple reality is that people in law enforcement are every bit as complex as patients and their family members. As angry as we might get about their decisions and actions some times we should

never forget that the saint one minute can become the sinner the next, and each of us is capable of exactly the same things.
By Anonymous

How has your encounter with the legal system changed you and those close to you? How do you see the world differently now?

It has turned in to a lion defending its young. I feel that i am my brothers advocate and I have to do anything in my power to see that he is treated with dignity, and is provided with the same legal rights as someone without a mental illness, and that means speaking on my brothers behalf and providing the court with my families testimonies on events and such.

Yes, I see the world different in the way that sometimes it's about money & politics. That my brother might not get a fair trial or be judged fairly because he has a mental illness and usually family members are not present because the attorneys or their assistants do not contact family members to let them know about court hearings or something important that might help their client (your family member with mental illness)... so you as a family member have to keep up to date on things and investigate & call and ask questions, get information, do the research.
By Anonymous

If you had to go through this process all over again, what would you do differently and why?

Get involved more. Take the initiative to get the contact information of the person who is representing your sibling or get the court date & time by checking with the court house in your city. Be your sibling's advocate, no one knows him better than the family, and might be able to get the judge to get him help instead of just incarcerating him due to not making the correct decission or ruling based on the lack of information presented.

By grome_420

Making a Living

Things that happened

What do you do for a living and how long have you been at it?

I was a technical writer for computer software systems for 23 years. I am now retired.
By NAMISD.1.4i

What happened with your work when you first encountered this condition?

During two bouts of clinical depression, I lost two contract jobs, and two permanent jobs, because I couldn't function at the level required and I was too stressed.
By NAMISD.1.4i

How has this condition impacted your career path?

Being bipolar, I think I jumped around a lot. I dropped out of my Ph.D. program, joined a career path unrelated to my education, and changed jobs about every year. I hit a massive manic period after my divorce, wound up working myself out of a high level job in IT and into owning a small IT business. Not that being manic is good but sometimes it helps achieve things. I don't think I could have done that without my mania keeping me fired up, full of energy all night, sneaking off to meetings with potential clients and partners as I put down the foundation for what would become my company.

That was before I was diagnosed and I was amazed at how much I could accomplish. But mania ultimately turns around, after building up so much momentum I almost lost my company going through a severe period of depression.

Managing my illness and my cycles translates directly into how well I do now. When I'm stable, everything is stable, my employees work smoothly, my clients pay smoothly, projects seem to get done on time etc. When I've had break through episodes, employees leave, it becomes more difficult to deal with clients, everything slips.
By NAMISD.1.1d

A New Definition of Career
I was diagnosed with bipolar disorder at age 19. I earned a bachelor's degree from UCSD in literature and writing at 22, but even with my education, it is a stretch to say that I've ever had a traditional career. In the past, my bipolar symptoms have undermined my consistency, stress-tolerance, and memory. It is safer to say that I've "worked in different fields," including non-profit, medical research, business, and academia. I've done admin, writing, marketing, tutoring, and more.

However, none of these jobs are what I would consider a "career," which to me implies a "normal" white collar job with a decent salary and a modicum of prestige. Because in our society a "career" is the ticket to mainstream acceptance, and because I don't have one, it has been all that much harder to stay stable and on track with my recovery. Most people find some sort of structure and identity and self esteem in their career, as well as some sense of belonging--and money--and I have had to find these things elsewhere. Yet, it is imperative to stay within my limits and not expose myself to excessive stress, pressure, or inappropriate expectations. This is a job in and of itself.

My solution to this conundrum--to work without overworking--has a two-fold solution in my life. First, I work part-time at a community college as a writing tutor, and second, I volunteer with NAMI (National Alliance on Mental Illness), a powerful, national advocacy group advancing the interests of people affected by mental illness. In doing so, I have a great deal of flexibility, and I can generally focus my energies on activities where I have a high aptitude. With NAMI, I have done writing, editing, public speaking, event planning, film producing, and fund raising. I can choose when, how, and how much I work, and if I don't want to, I don't have to work at all.

As my health improves, I learn more and more, and I can do more and more. Although I don't have designs on the white collar career, I know that I am moving forward and keeping my skills as current as I can. Seeing myself do things I never thought I could do brings great joy.

More important, I've found that doing something for love, not money, is rewarding on a profound level. Although the traditional career may or may not be in my future, I know that there will always be a venue for me to express my talents and my passion for social change. For that, I can thank NAMI.

By NAMISD.1.6h

How candid can you be about your condition with your boss and those you work with?

When I was in the depths of my depression, I had to be candid with my bosses, because I could not function adequately. I lost those jobs. Since I have recovered, I do not tell my bosses about my depression. I do tell colleagues who are open with me about their mental illness if I think in doing so it would help them. I have

106

done that with colleagues several times and it has helped both of us.
By NAMISD.1.4i

Things you learned

What have you done to successfully adapt your work to accommodate the realities of this condition?

I did not further stress myself out by trying to get into management or play office politics. I focused on writing excellent technical computer manuals. I also did not work all hours or weekends unless I was meeting a deadline. Then I did it for a short time knowing there was an end coming.
By NAMISD.1.4i

What have you found to be the best way to protect your health in the face of a demanding job?

Not let myself get talked into working too hard or doing something I don't believe in. I learned to stand up for myself and tell people when I felt too much work was being piled on or when I knew I couldn't or shouldn't work extra hours.
By NAMISD.1.4i

What communication methods or strategies have best helped you deal with those you work with?

I talk frankly, openly, and honest about what works for me and what doesn't work for me in terms of my job. I only share my bouts with clinical depression with my colleagues if I feel it would help them or me. I keep my focus on my job and doing an excellent job of writing computer manuals. I have learned over the years not to be as sensitive to other people's perceptions as I once was, and not to take things at work personally.

By NAMISD.1.4i

Daily Life

Things that happened

What's the hardest part of your day?

I'm answering this question as an OCD survivor.

As I recall, the hardest part of my day....., was every moment, from the time I opened my eyes in the morning to the time I hopefully drifted off to sleep at night.

My OCD revolved around germs. So, in the most tortuous time in this disease, I couldn't seem to touch anything without either disinfecting the object and/or washing my hands with soap, bleach, lysol....anything that I hoped might kill the germ. I imagined all kinds of diseases lurking...ready for me to acquire & then pass on to my family & close friends. It seems that was the biggest stress... the possiblility that my not disinfecting, might cause harm to someone else.

This, of course, took over my entire life, and made it virtually impossible to lead whatever a "normal" life would be.
By Anonymous

What's the biggest change mental illness brings to your life?

Since I deal with mild depression, I find it is worse some days than others. The hardest thing I deal with is lack of motivation to do anything. Some days I wake up full of concentrated energy and I can be focused and get a lot done. Other days I can barely get out of bed. I've learned to accept those kinds of days and I no longer beat myself up over them. I just appreciate the days that I can function. The hardest parts of the bad day is the downward spiral of negative thinking. Sometimes I get myself to the point that I am unable to see anything positive about my life at all. I've learned not to make any big decisions on bad days and to do nurturing things allowing for plenty of quiet time when possible. I will often want to sleep a lot on those days. Interestingly enough, I can rarely remember how bad things seemed the next day. I often think to myself, what WAS so bad?

Overall, I've learned patience, forgiveness and the ability to acknowledge that it is temporary. I do take Lexapro now which has helped. There are fewer bad days.
By NAMISD.1.2e

Being able to know your feelings and understand when you are in a postion that is hazardous to you or others/or a position that is risky. I have not done this, but it has been suggested to me that I keep a mood journal because this way I can be aware of my feelings throughout the day and when I start to shift I can go back and see what I was doing differntly or the same and can assess the situation from there.
By Kia426

What role do family, friends, faith, and work contribute to your ability to cope with this condition?

My faith plays a huge role in dealing with the mental illness of my son. I have tried to do everything I know of to help my son but, ultimately, I trust God with the outcome of this situation. I have prayed for healing but also for guidance to know how best to help my son and I

110

have received answers to my prayers. My son is not cured but I remain hopeful that he will improve over time.

I believe we should not hide the fact of our loved one's mental illness - that only contributes to the stigma. So I am up front about my son's illness as if it were any other illness I would share about. If, after having shared things with my friends, I find that some of them are not sympathetic or supportive, then I discontinue talking about my son with those friends. I only share with the friends that I know care about me and my son. Some of them have been very supportive and helpful.

When I worked, it was good to have something to do that required a lot of my attention and focus. Now that I'm retired, I have found other activities that require my involvement and find that, while I am participating in them, I am not thinking about my son's mental illness which is good.
By NAMISD.1.5d

My family has given me unconditional love and acceptance since I was 17 and started with my depressive symptoms. They have stood by me while I was undiagnosed for another 17 years, and throughout the years thereafter.

I have lost old friends along the way as I became more and more disabled with my mental illness and experienced feelings of shame, embarrassment, inadequacy, worthlessness, uselessness, and thought myself a failure. I have felt lonely, isolated, confused, and abandoned. Talking to old friends and acquaintances is difficult. I have never been to a high school reunion. On the other hand, I've also made new friends along the way who are in the mental health field and accepting of mental illnesses.

Faith gives me my goal in life - to live a life with genuine vitality, purpose, and gratitude. Obstacles will be thrown

111

at me, but it is imperative that I do not fear the challenges because in the long-run, I believe those challenges promote my growth. I believe we were created in Spirit to be interdependent, to assist, support, and encourage one another to find our purpose, seek our service, and deal with our challenges in order to make a difference in the world. Our true purpose in life is to make a difference in the lives of others. To inspire others to love, to encourage them to dream, and to empower them to keep hope alive are among the most blessed of all achievements.

By Anonymous

Things you learned

How do you deal with the stigma associated with mental illness?

When I was actually going through the major part of my OCD, I really wasn't sure what was happening to me. You really question what's real (germwise), & what is not.

When I finally found a Doctor who REALLY knew how to treat this illness (and I tried many), I still wasn't ready to talk about OCD to my friends & some of my family...you just "know" they'll think you're "nuts." Thank God, I had my mom's shoulders to lean on. What I didn't realize is that they all knew there was something wrong, anyway...but how could I explain something I was so embarrassed about and didn't understand?

So, it took many years of behavioral therapy along with Prozac/Buspar...before I could try to deal with the stigma of mental illness. My doctor, Dr. C., had told me that most of her patients weren't ready to talk about their illness until they were much healthier. Very true with me as well.

When I get in a conversation with someone who is grappling with this topic or even making jokes about mental illness, I try my best to educate them. I may even share some of my personal experience if it seems safe, and if they're really interested, I direct them to NAMI.
By Anonymous

Of all the adaptations you've made to deal with this condition which has been the most helpful?

Adaption of my expectations of myself has been the hardest but the most helpful thing I've done to live well with bipolar disorder. For many years, I tried living with a self concept that did not take into account that I had a mental illness. I always tried working myself too hard. I drank too much. I tried to "keep up" with people socially and economically. Because of my behavior--overdoing it--I would become sick and spend about a month in the hospital annually, year after year. It took my a long time to give up on a false notion of myself and to live with a more comfortable self image, albeit slower and with a lower profile. Since I've done that, though, my life is so much better. I still have mood swings, but I don't get really, really ill or go to the hospital. A lot of the time I spent "keeping up" with others is spent on staying well, and now I don't judge myself for just being the me I need to be.
By NAMISD.1.6h

Have any of the adjustments you've made produced unexpected consequences or benefits? If so, what are they?

Ten years of volunteer work for NAMI-NCSDC (faith and friends) has significantly contributed to my ability to cope with my condition. I have come to believe that

113

volunteerism is spiritual activism in its highest form. Whenever I give with an open heart without any expectation of receiving in return, I become love and compassion in action. There is a deep sense of joy in giving to others when they are filled with knowledge and hope. When I am stable enough in my illness to act in a volunteer position, I am filled with a deep sense of purpose and meaning. My life becomes significant and my message meaningful.

By Anonymous

What's the best advice that someone ever gave you about living with a mental illness?

My best advice is keep on going. I want to work but then I am afraid that my medical conditions and my mental illness will make it hard for me. Sometimes I think just working on me is a lot. Sometimes I think it is ok to just volunteer. I feel like things can be hard to do, but, I think my best advice is to find a doctor you like and trust. Then be honest with him and let him help you.

When things are tough, I sometimes daydream about how I could be like a hero and sometimes like what I want. I listen to everyone's problems because it helps me see that maybe mine are not so bad. I guess everyone has bad times and even though it seems like forever, it isn't. Think about this, if I had succeeded in giving up, I wouldn't have been able to be here today. It is like a cake, sometimes you gotta wait for it to bake up and get done cooking before you know how it turns out. It could be like a big fat cookie. If it's good, you get to eat it, if not, make another one and if that one isn't good then make something else. Eventually you will make something that is good. Sometimes it takes a long time like a puzzle. But one day it's done and then it is really nice, just like you.

Life is a mystery, we get clues along the way, but the big picture doesn't always make sense until we are ready to see it. Be good to yourself, my therapist tells me that a lot and you know what? I like that now. Ok I am not rich, I am not super smart, but I am me and that is good. Sometimes I make a small treat and sometimes I pretend that I am on a big vacation, I put my favorite things around me, make a snack and away I go.

Be good to yourself, you deserve it. My life is up and down it isn't always easy, but now I have made some good friends and I know they really care about me. This didn't happen overnight, trust me. I am 51 and I had to wait for what seemed like an eternity to get where I am, so please give yourself time to get there. Sometimes we go through bad things so we can really appreciate the good things that come our way. I once heard on tv, that pain is like giving birth, you go through all this pain to get you ready for something really good. I think that means that a baby is born but causes pain because the baby is special, so maybe that is why the guy said that. I know things can be really hard, but do whatever it takes to get through it. Don't give up. There is a place for you because I never thought I would be happy and now even though I still struggle everyday, I am mostly happy for the most part ok? Give yourself plenty of time and lots of love.

The best advice I got came from my mom and dad, they said be yourself. If you aren't you and someone doesn't like you then you can't just say, oops, that wasn't really me, but if you are you and someone doesn't like you then it's not your fault. If you are you then you are true to yourself and lots of people like people that are real, there are enough actors in the world. That is the best advice I ever got, because, I have learned to love me. I am me and I can be happy with just being me. I can change if I don't like something about me, and I don't have to hide.
By Anonymous

Use your experience to help others through similiar struggles, and remeber that you hardships and pain will make you a strong individual.
By Anonymous

Self-Image

Things that happened

How do you see yourself today, and how has that image been changed by this illness?

I see myself as a consumer today. The term consumer does not bother me much as long as I am not limited by it. The reason for this is I also see myself as a provider. Lots of times I have shared my experience with other peers to help them on their way, not to mention coordinating the Peer to Peer classes I have been doing for a year.

The illness has definitely changed my identity. Before I was diagnosed, I had no idea what the terms consumer and provider meant. Mental illness, furthermore, was not even in my reality and now it is my reality. Acceptance of this fact continues to help me overcome trials in life.
By NAMISD.1.4h

I am much more self-confident now. I don't worry as much about what people think of me. I have much more loving relationships with my children and the rest of my family. I don't "sweat the small stuff" much anymore. I try to enjoy what each day brings me. I also try to grieve when I need to grieve, and be joyful when I am. I don't "stuff" my feelings as much anymore. I try to express them honestly and then let them go. I had to do a great deal of soul-searching as a result of my severe depression, because I lost so much and I really couldn't function. Through therapy, 12-step groups, my church, reading, and many other healthy mental practices, I really did totally redo my image of myself, and, therefore, I believe I am a much better person to be around.
By NAMISD.1.4i

What or who has the biggest influence on how you see yourself and how you live your life? Why is that influence so significant?

My friends and family were the biggest influence on how I learned to see myself, treat myself, and express myself. As a teenager and in my early twenties I struggled a great deal with taking care of myself and respecting and being kind to myself. I expressed my anger and fears by cutting on myself and having suicidal thoughts. It took me many years to move beyond that treatment of myself and to learn to respect my mind and body. As of today it has been about three years since I last hurt myself through self-injury and I am very thankful and proud of myself. I still have many scars left over from those years of pain, but now they just bring back memories of where my mental illness started and how far I have come since then with my recovery.

My family and friends were the ones who reminded me many times that I was a person worth protecting and keeping safe. They spent time with me and worked hard to help me see that I was not alone and never would be alone. Slowly I began to share more and more of my inner feelings with them and that helped a lot with my personal struggles. I also learned that not only was it important for me to know I was not alone and needed others to feel good about myself, but it was important for me to know that there were others in the world who needed me to feel good about themselves too. Finding a balance between giving and needing is difficult, but I enjoy the challenge and the experiences that go along with it. All in all though, I must be honest and say that without my family and friends I don't think I would be alive and here today to share my story. I am thankful to them all and express my gratitude every day just by living well.

By NAMISD.1.5g

What have you gained and lost as a result of this illness?

I have lost the belief that I am invincible! I am have realized that I am human. I sure do miss my "super powers", but I would not trade the compassion and understanding I have gained for others with a mental illness. I have gained the power to change the life of another person who is suffering by giving them hope. I "know" the depth of their pain, despair, hopelessness, and isolation. I have made it through and so can they.

By Anonymous

To best answer this question I need to give you an understanding of how much time it has taken in my life to gain awareness of my disease, seek help, accept my diagnosis, and continue my life with renewed understanding and self acceptance. As I look back throughout the span of my 50+ years, I think I always carried depression and sadness as unwanted companions. I was born into a post WWII family situation that brought it's own complications for me. My father returned from the war to a bride he really didn't know that well. My father's strict German background continually clashed with my mother's carefree Irish spirit. As I look back now it must have been hard for these young parents to struggle with their early marriage, their own dreams, and two young children at the same time. I felt loved but always felt that was conditional.

Physical appearance was a key point of acceptability to my parents. My parents were of average weight, at least in the early years, but apparently had family members with significant weight issues that embarrased them. With my genetic influence my own weight was frequently 25+ pounds over the ideal. My parents worries that I might became obese and therefore an embarrasement to them became very apparent. What could only be described now as abusive treatment, I was continually weighed, thrust in front of doctors, and shamed about my appearance. I was frequently told no wants to be around a fat girl. I wasn't fat, but their perception of the truth seemed easier to believe.

Despite this struggle at home for acceptance, I was a popular girl, always a leader or elected officer of clubs and programs, and intelligent enough to be selected to National Honorary Society. However, the pervasive treatment and lack of approval left me continually sad and lonely. Perhaps the early strains of depression had already begun, to this day I am not sure.

College life was a lonely, frightening experience. I was far from home, young, and still aching that my physical appearance (despite being quite pretty and of normal weight at this point) would somehow not make me acceptable. Things went from bad to worse, I narrowly missed being a victim of date rape, flunked out of two successive schools, and arrived at my third school full of doubt, depressed and very unsure of myself. I managed to find a group of women that were accepting, loving, and each just trying to deal with their own issues of making good life choices.

I did graduate, remet the wonderful boyfriend that made my teenage years bearable, married him, and found myself quickly teaching school and discovering the ups and downs of young married life while my husband struggled through professional school. The depression that was quickly enveloping me still was so omnipresent and I attributed that to my disgust with a once again increased weight....that it was an issue of weight, not that possibly I had a mental illness. I knew nothing of that possibility and certainly spoke to no one,

Now I realize the classic signs of depression. I was continually physical ill, I pulled away from friends and colleagues, and finally in an instant felt there was only one solution, I swallowed a bottle of aspirin. I'm not sure I thought of this as a suicide attempt, but rather just a way to escape the very intense pain of feeling so miserable. The following days of hospitilization were embarrasing, frightening, and left my husband and I unable to truly understand what just happend. Most important however was secrecy. I told no one and to this day only a few very trusted loved ones know this story. Quick trips to psychologists further terrified me and I left without any help and tried to plug ahead with my life.

I have a very keen ability to pull myself together, be resilient, and move forward with my life. So I did...my husband and I continued with carreers, had children, and had by all considerations a wonderful, happy life together. Unfortunately, sadness, and uncertainity frequently were companions. As my career became brighter, the demands of a busy family increased, social, and community involvement increased, my health went through several significant major issues of disease and surgery and trying to move forward. All throughout this time my despair over weight issues became a major eating disorder and depression.

Realizing at this point I might really have some major problems to deal with, I began to trust my wonderful husband and a few friends to confide in. Unfortunately at this time my parents in their advanced ages were becoming quite ill and also required my attention. It was the perfect storm. I sunk into a major depression and could not get out of bed. I sought help and finally confronted a disease that most likely had its roots long before in my early childhood. Thanks to my loving family, excellent counselling, and effective medication I began my recovery.

So, what have I lost as a result of this illness? I lost so much time, so much of my life, so much time I didn't understand, or I was too embarrased, too scared people would discover all my issues and shun me. I lost the vibrant knowledge and security of a good self concept that would have most definitely enhanced my life and made me so much stronger. What I gained as I now think about it however is a much deeper appreciation and knowledge about many topics. I finally realize through genetics, I have been dealing with mental illness and coping as well as I could my whole life. I gained a true appreciation of what a strong woman I am. My own knowledge and my issues, stories, experiences define who I am and I feel hopefully have made me the effective wife, parent, friend, and teacher that I am. Through NAMI, I have developed more self respect and self love and have regained my love of wanting to help others. I continually use this knowledge and have been able to offer care for others dealing with mental illness, including my own son, and others in my family who were never diagnosed but I now realize had their own mental health issues.

Mental illness is a very real part of who I am, but the biggest gain in all of this is I reclaimed my true self...what a wonderful gift!!
By Anonymous

Wow, well, this is an interesting question as I hadn't thought too much about what I have actually gained from having mental illness. My thoughts are focused mainly on what I have lost because of it. I have major depression, so my thoughts tend to naturally sway towards the negative in most circumstances. I can easily tell you what I have lost by having this disease that plagues the mind and often the heart and soul to boot. I have lost a job due to a nervous breakdown--a job that found me making more money than I ever had before, climbing the corporate ladder of "success" and then plummeting down to the very bottom of that mountain it had taken me so long to climb in the first place.

I have lost friends and some ties with family due to my isolating behaviors and others just not understanding, or wanting to try. I have lost dignity, independence, money, time, and, for a while there, I even thought I had lost myself. Some days I still feel that way. Have I really lost myself in all of this? What is the essence of me and does it

122

still exist as I am propped up by medications and therapy sessions? Will I ever "get over" this disease? What is true recovery anyway?

Some days I definitely have more questions than answers. Most days.

But if I turn it around and try to see what I have gained from having this illness, well, let's see...I guess I have gained some perspective. I cannot work fulltime and am on disability right now and, though I don't make very much money, it certainly has given me time to reflect on what I think "success" is. I have had the time to smell the roses, take in the sunsets, and thoroughly enjoy even the most simple aspects of my pet dog. Sometimes I just like to lay my head against her side, hear her heartbeat and feel her breathing. Sometimes that very action is enough to quell my anxiety, if only for a few minutes.

The few friendships that I do have now are very special to me and have deepened. I feel that when I talk with a friend, I really talk and don't just shoot the breeze with meaningless chitchat. We actually connect and that makes a difference. It's nice to have one or two people in my life who really "get" me.

The work I can do is precious to me in many ways. Since it takes so much effort to do any kind of work these days, what I can produce is to be cherished and my efforts not taken for granted. I feel this from the people I do get to work with; I do feel appreciated by them and feel that the work I am doing is making a positive difference in the world--something I never felt before when I was on that shaky corporate ladder.

I guess the last thing I can think of that I have gained from having mental illness is guts and gumption. While many, many times I have wanted to give up, give in and check out, I am still alive, still here, and still breathing. I am still putting one foot in front of the other, as small and as backwards as those steps may be sometimes. I have learned that life is not for the faint of heart, yet sometimes it's the faint of heart that get to live it more than others in all its raw reality, full color and oceanic emotions.

And maybe, just maybe, that's okay too.
By Anonymous

I felt like a fraud most of my life- putting on a good face-hiding the real me. I had no self respect.

When I became symptomatic, I lost the ability to concentrate, so I coudn't do my job. I lost my relationship with my family- I lost my identity.

I learned that I have to manage stress, not take on too much and tell the truth.

When I started volunteering for and speaking in IOOV, the "In Our Own Voice" Program I gained back my self respect. I was faithful to my treatment and got more stable in my recovery. I was able to reestablish a good relationship with my children and grandchildren and start a new career as IOOV Coordinator, State and National Trainer.

I have learned that I have a lot to share and my life today has purpose. I like who I am.
By NAMISD.1.4c

Has this condition caused you to see yourself privately as being different from what the world sees? If so, what's the difference and how do you deal with it?

I guess the best way to explain this is that at one time in my life I could say it was like a book shelf. God was on top, then the next shelf down was my family. The next shelf down had my teachers and police and doctors. Then was my friends on the fourth shelf down. I was at the bottom. I don't know why exactly but I felt like I was missing something that everybody else had. I told my therapist and she helped me move slowly up the book case and now I feel good. I am not sure where I am on the book case, but I am kinda mostly in with my family and sometimes I am really happy and I feel like no matter where I am on the book shelf, I am important. If I fall off the book shelf like when I am sad or when I have a bad day, I know that I can rearrange the bookshelf. I can put what I want on the book shelf and I can move the people on the book shelf around if I want to, but I mostly like that I can dust it off and start over if I want to.

I keep the bottom shelf empty so if I am unhappy and I remember I can put my sad, or mad face on the bottom and move it up again when I feel better. I don't know how I ever felt like everything on a book shelf, but I think it was just a way I could see me and the world. Now, most of the time I can be on the top shelves, now it took a long time, but I made it and I worked hard at it. I needed lots of help to do that and I am still working on it, but I like that I can move it around. I really like when I can be on the same shelf as everone I like because I feel like I am as good as them too.

My real friends tell me the truth and they always make me feel about me. Some of my best friends get to be on my family shelf because they treat me so nice and I consider them like family. I also have a special shelf for my co-workers and my pets. My favorite shelf is the shelf with treats on it, like being good to me, or doing something special with a friend. I never thought I could move around the book shelf but I was wrong and now I can find it helpful when I think about where I see me and what my friends tell me they see. My book shelf has never fallen over yet.
By Anonymous

I think the world sees me as a weak person because of my mental illness. As part of the stigma of mental illness, I have chosen to become an advocate of the mentally ill and work for NAMI in educating the public through the In Our Own Voices ("IOOV") and other NAMI consumer programs. Hopefully through education comes the knowledge that breaks down the barriers of the shame and disgrace that comes with a diagnosis of being mentally ill.

By Anonymous

Do you find yourself trying to keep up a public façade? If so, why and how do you maintain it?

Why Tell

I still wonder when to share that I have bipolar disorder and when to keep it to myself. I wonder who to tell, and where, and how much. As with all things, the understanding of the power of self disclosure, as well as its parameters, is gradual, so I wonder away.

No matter what, I know the choice to share is mine and mine alone. In some instances, I keep quiet. Other times, I just plain lie. More and more, though, I choose to disclose. I choose to disclose for good reasons, like building intimacy, educating, or inspiring social change. Ultimately, though, I disclose for myself. By letting someone else know, I remind myself that I'm OK, that I have nothing to hide. I remind myself that I've got guts.

Most importantly, I remind the illness who's boss.

Of course, sometimes, the reason for keeping quiet is obvious.

On one occasion, I was at an In 'n Out drive thru. I ordered Combo #1, a Double Double animal style with fries and a medium drink. When I reached the window, I was prepared with the exact change, but when I went to give it to the clerk, my hands were shaking so badly from lithium tremors that it was a struggle to give her the money. The clerk, alarmed, yelled to her co-workers, "Hurry up! She's hypoglycemic!" Rather than correcting the clerk, I merely smiled and took my Johnny-on-the-spot, extra-hot Double Double. Yay! A bonus of being bipolar!

Naturally, there have been more delicate situations when I kept my diagnosis to myself. Years ago, I taught swing dancing at a local club and was a well-known figure within the swing community. I was at the club every week, except for a stretch of time when I had been in the hospital for a month because of a serious manic episode. My dance partner and close friends kept the reason for my absence hush hush. I was "taking time off" because I was "really, really busy."

When I returned to the club after my struggle with acute mania, I had lost 15 pounds and was extremely thin. My rapid weight loss was seen as a great accomplishment. I got round after round of compliments about how good I looked. How did I do it? I raved about my winning combination of "cardio and carrot juice." Lying did the trick. My reputation as a "normie" was safe.

As time went on, even though it could be risky letting people know my diagnosis, I gained something valuable by disclosing. Not only that, it seemed easier and easier to distinguish the right venue, the right time, and the right person to share with.

For three years, I worked in the insurance industry with my brother, an agent for a well-known company, and we shared our office with various real estate agents and other business people. The CEO of the real estate business was a former Captain of the US Navy, and there were signed photos of him posed with George Bush and Arnold Schwarzenegger in the lobby. People passed each other in the corridors with little or no connection, and though I got to know a few folks on a casual basis, in the first year or so, no one "knew."

Eventually, I decided to let someone in on my secret. I was talking to a real estate agent who I called "Positive Phil." Phil prided himself on being upbeat, and he always had something nice to say and was always a pleasure to talk to. We were buddies.

One day, Phil said that "everyone has a choice" about "whether it's going to be a good day or a bad day." He gave me his own version of The Power of Positive Thinking.

I took a chance. "Some people can't be positive all the time," I argued, "people like me, for example." I continued, "Phil, I'm bipolar...I get depressed sometimes, and that's a biological thing. It's not a choice. Clinical depression is a medical problem, an illness." Now, Phil knew me to be a cheerful, fun person. He was stunned for a moment, and then backpedaled, "I mean, when you can choose to make it a good day, it's a good day." We split the difference, and our friendship took a baby step forward. I felt that Phil knew me better, and accepted me, although his attitudes really did not change.

As it turns out, my interaction with Phil gave me more courage and set the stage for another office conversation with someone I had more invested in and more to lose.

Jerrod worked in property management. He was intelligent, quick-witted, and slightly cynical. We both grew up during the '80's and liked to swap stories about music and pop culture. Both with "real" day planners, we bonded over the sad rise of gadgetry and the erosion of face-to-face communication. Since Jerrod's office was near the kitchen, when I popped by to chat, I always had a cup of tea in one shaky hand.

One day, leaning on the doorpost of Jerrod's office, the tremors were particularly bad, and I almost spilled my tea. When he asked me what caused the shaking, I smiled and said, "I drink a lot of caffeine, and I take medication, which is not a great combination." He replied, "If you don't mind my asking, what kind of medication?" I admitted, "Well, the shaking is caused by lithium." His eyes lit up, "Lithium? You're bipolar?" I nodded. Jerrod invited me into his office, shut the door, and told me what it was like to grow up with a mother who was bipolar and wouldn't take her medication.

Jerrod and I became friends, but more importantly, I began to realize the primary value in telling others about my condition. Although I became closer to Jerrod, which was a plus, that wasn't really the central point for me. The point was finding that place in myself that was unafraid, that was willing to put something vulnerable out there and take the chance of being rejected. During this process, I discovered that sharing counteracted the illness' power to instill shame and self-stigma.

Despite the benefits of being bold, however, rejection was always a possible outcome and not something I relished. The greatest challenge for me was telling someone in a romantic relationship about my diagnosis. In 2002, I started dating Travis. We hit it off right away. Travis fell into the enviable category of a "great guy," a great, "normal" guy. He was handsome, smart, funny, and considerate. We had gone out on a couple of dates, and it was apparent from the get go that we had fun together and seemed to be compatible, although we were opposites. He was stable, linear, practical, technical, military, and mainstream in his thinking. I liked him enormously and decided I should tell him about my illness before I started liking him even more.

Travis and I were at my apartment chatting when I announced that I had to tell him something important. "I'm bipolar," I admitted warily, expecting shock and rejection. "OK." he said, "C'mon...let's go." We left for his friend's party where he introduced me as his girlfriend. Travis didn't learn what the word bipolar meant until a couple of weeks later when a friend reacted, "Dude, are you crazy? Bipolar! She's crazy!" Travis didn't care; the damage had been done.

Six months later, Travis learned what bipolar disorder really meant when he had to call the police to have me hospitalized for manic psychosis. I had been awake for days, and Travis took sick days to follow me around town in the middle of the night, keeping me safe until I exhausted him.

I am glad that Travis was armed with knowledge of the illness because unprepared, he never would have had the ability to weather the horrible transformation of his girlfriend. Luckily, he stayed, and I started the journey of recovery in earnest. That was seven years ago.

At this point in my life, now that my recovery is steady, disclosure is something even more important to me. I must remind myself that the disorder is not who I am, nor is it my dirty secret, nor is it my vocation, nor is it my hobby, nor does it make me special. Bipolar disorder is an illness, albeit a fascinating one, but an illness just the same.

Ultimately, telling someone I have bipolar disorder is one small way of transcending my self-judgment. Revealing my diagnosis is not just about "growing intimacy," or "educating others," or even "social progress," although those things are a positive byproducts of openness.

When I have the courage to speak up, to possibly be rejected by someone else, I know I have the courage to accept myself. When I can reduce the power of the disorder by shedding light on it, I have the courage to keep going. When I can admit that I have a medical illness, I have the courage to continue my recovery. When I can tell somebody else, it means I have the courage to tell the illness to leave me be.

That's why I tell. I tell for me.
By NAMISD.1.6h

Is there anything else that has happened to you or that you've experienced in this area that you would like to share?

When I was first diagnosed with Bi-Polar, I asked a old friend if she had suspected anything. She said "I never knew which one of you I was going to see, but I loved you both."

That staement made me feel like I was really OK even with a mental illness.
By NAMISD.1.4c

Things you learned

How have you redefined your life and the quality of your life following the diagnosis of this illness?

Following my diagnosis, I found a trusted psychologist, and began the often painful process of putting the building blocks of who I was as a person back together. I needed to "relive" some painful secrets that included childhood rejection, incest attempts, abusive relationships, and most certainly, as a result, poor self esteem. The work was physically draining, so deeply troubling and difficult. Journaling and visualization techniques helped me remember the secrets, face them, discuss them with my doctor and learn how to release them. I was determined that my past was just that. I also adopted the philosophy that any "irregular" people in my past did their best with the tools they were given in their own lives, which probably weren't the best always... I wanted to quit so very often...I was sure the burden was too hard and that I couldn't make it through to the other side. I'll always remember, my doctor told me...I will have the faith for both of us that you will get healthy, hold onto that until you see it as well...and I did.

With my doctor's help, I created lists of my wonderful qualities and all the qualities of life that I wanted....hobbies, travels to take...small comforts that I had quit giving time to, like drawing. I reclaimed my inner health guru and became a physical exercise enthusiast, creating for the first time my own personal home gym. I adopted a much more healthy approach to eating that eventually led me to becoming a vegetarian. I reconnected with friends, and to my amazement realized they were always my friends but were just waiting for my "return." Most importantly I created a new balance of life with a more comfortable pace of career, time enjoying all my hobbies, and basking in family love and good times with friends.

My life quality would not have become this rich without first facing my diagnosis, securing help, taking medication, trusting caring medical professionals, and realizing I could indeed have the life that I wanted. I am a deeply religious woman and still feel God is central to all the amazing qualities and gifts and even obstacles in my life. I believe once we know who we are, what we want, it is up to us to reach for it. No one else can do it for you and you need to quit blaming others for what you may not have received in your your youth, or the frustrations and hardships, and instead move forward and claim the rich life you deserve...we all have that right and that power.

So has my life changed...you bet..I now live in full color. Of course I need to always remember my personal requirements for continued mental recovery, such as exercise, a healthy diet, a balance of work and personal time, faith, and love. I am so very lucky.
By Anonymous

I have redefined my life in terms of how I interact with people and treat people, rather than what material or professional successes I have. The quality of my life now depends on the little things--interacting with a grandchild, helping a friend, being there for a child. I get much joy from conversations with friends, being out in nature, or reading good books. I used to feel I always had to be productive and be a model wife and mother. I have learned how to be. I used to think about the past or future all the time. Now I have learned to stay in the present as much as possible and enjoy what is right in front of me.

By Anonymous

What are your goals, dreams and expectations now and how are they different from before the onset of this condition?

After not touching a drum set in more than 20 years, he has now, for the last 2 years, been teaching his nephew, our grandson, to play the drums. At the same time, he is regaining the skills that he left behind all those years ago, and has just purchased a complete set of drums in the form of pads, so that he can practice and improve his skills without disturbing his fellow condominium dwellers.

Although he has not fulfilled the promise held for him before the onset of his illness, we are very proud of his achievements, and continue to support him in fulfilling any of the dreams that he currently aspires to.

He still struggles with the vagaries of the Social Security system as they periodically inform him that he has earned too much and arbitrarily stop his checks. This happens in spite of his continued diligence in trying to keep his earnings within the guidelines. He is continually learning how to successfully deal with these situations, in spite of the stress they cause.

By Anonymous

What have you learned about yourself and the people close to you?

Not everyone is going to understand what you are going through. Some may even avoid you. Friends, family, co-workers may give you well intentioned advice or suggestions. Some if these include "Just snap out of it", "Wear brighter colors", "Exercise more", etc. My silent response was "Gee, don't you think if I could snap out of it I would?" Wow, do you think they told the person with diabetes to "Just snap out of it"? The lesson I learned was "Forgive them for they know not what they say." I learned the importance of "Ask, Seek, Knock." We need to ask and seek help from professionals not amateurs. Then we need to actively participate in our recovery. When we get to the door we need to knock to get in....standing outside the door silent and waiting for it to open usually doesn't work very well.
By Anonymous

Initally I learned how ignorant we all were about mental illness and how much in denial we were. Some people close to me are still in denial, but many people have understood and come around. I have learned that I'm a survivor, that I'm actually very resilient, and that people do love me. I am far from perfect, and that's okay. I can try to do better and that's okay, too. I am really proud of my brother and his wife. Their young daughter (5) was engaging in excessive hand-washing. They immediately recognized that something was wrong and took her to a mental health professional. With medication and counseling--and knowledge of the people closest to her--she has excelled in her studies and sports, and is studying to be an architect in college.
By Anonymous

As a person, how have you changed? How have you grown?

At 50 I thought my life was over. Today at 66 I look forward to new experiences. I'm much easier on myslef- I've learned to change my negative thoughts (most of the time) to positive nourishing ones. I tell the truth and keep my word. I still have trouble with setting bounderies, but am getting better and I'm enjoying the process.
By NAMISD.1.4c

Has this condition caused the awakening of any parts of you that you didn't know you had?

Very much so. Before I accepted that I had a mental illness, I had to accept pain as a part of life. Now that I am a paraplegic due to a suicide attempt six and a half years ago, the pain is undeniable. Thankfully I can manage that pain which helps me combat the symptoms of Bipolar Disorder, which continue nonetheless.

The journey has also awakened my spirituality as I discovered that I love to worship God through song and fellowship with others. I believe the Bible in 1st John 4:15 when it is written, "If anyone acknowledges that Jesus is the Son of God, God lives in him and he in God." Therefore, I can experience God internally on my own as well as corporately by praising Jesus with others. Before accepting the mental illness, I did not have a working relationship with God nor did I know about the joys of going to church.
By NAMISD.1.4h

I am a much stronger, more resilient person than I thought I was. I also consider myself to be more courageous.
By Anonymous

135

What do you tell yourself about yourself, and how do you keep that 'self-talk' healthy?

Throughout the many years that I've been dealing with my mental illness I think the hardest part is being kind to myself and finding ways to think positively about myself. All my life I have been a very giving and caring person. I think that helps me a lot. I have found that what really seems to make my life enjoyable is my ability to give to others. I know what it feels like to be alone, misunderstood, or singled out and because I've experienced those feelings myself. I have the power to help others get beyond those feelings and think better of themselves. I frequently remind myself of that ability in order to feel better about myself. Having my symptoms and diagnosis has led me on a path that is different from many people, but I think in some ways I am actually grateful for my mental illness because it has taught me to live a life of giving, sharing, and caring. I think that kind of education is far more important than school. I feel good about myself every time I am reminded of my abilities by talking to a friend, volunteering, or even just making someone smile. As long as I talk to myself kindly and remind myself that I can change the world despite being ill I stay healthy and happy.

By NAMISD.1.5g

One of my oldest patterns is to tell myself that no one loves me. After a fight with a daughter, I recently said that to my spiritual director. She said, "That is a lie! You have talked a lot about your children, and I can tell that you have a deep relationship with them." So I tell that to myself now, anytime I'm feeling unloved. Also, when I get anxious about money, I tell myself that I've made it so far, and with God's help and my community's help, I will keep making it through.

By NAMISD.1.4i

The Impact of
Mental Illness on
Relationships

Things that happened

What are the kindest, most helpful or most significant things that someone has done for you to help you with your mental illness or the mental illness of someone close to you?

My son's crime had the potential of tearing our family apart but it did not. My faith in God kept me strong. Although impossible to understand why such terrible things happen in life I found strength in my faith and in people who share faith in the Lord. The kindest and most significant things said and done were that people told us they would pray for us and our son. These were not empty words. I know we had many family and friends praying for us over a two year period. The other kind acts were my family and friends just letting me cry in front of them without seeming to be uncomfortable. They just let me grieve. In the end our son was found not guilty by reason of insanity and placed in a state hospital where his recovery has been remarkable. Prayer worked. In addition to prayer, the kindest acts anyone can offer is an attempt to understand that mental illness is out of one's control and to not pass judgment, no matter what may arise out of the mental illness.
By Anonymous

Has this condition brought you into new relationships or friendships, and if so, how and with whom?

One of the positives about fully accepting mental illness has been the new relationships and friendships that have occurred as a result. Once we discovered the wonderful organization called NAMI our circle of caring friends immediately increased. From the first moment I registered for the Family to Family education program, I felt accepted, welcomed, and encouraged to realize this was a special organization where I could fully relax and not worry about the stigma of the illness. For the very first time, my husband and I could cry, vent, and discuss all our issues and worries and frustrations knowing people surrounding us knew exactly our struggles and wanted to support us and sustain us with their own stories of hope and recovery.

In quick succession we were given much relevant information about mental illness, support groups to attend, and found a wonderful new psychiatrist that finally gave us an accurate diagnosis for our son. Our circle of sustaining friendships continued to grow. I became very involved as an instructor for the family education programs and eventually joined the staff of NAMI San Diego. My work with the organization gives me so much more than vibrant work to be involved with, it gives me friendships that foster my happiness and offset the burdens of mental illness that do occur. It has also become extremely important to "play this forward." I want to extend friendship and knowledge about mental illness and NAMI to everyone I come in contact with. I feel my whole world has opened up and the stigma of mental illness that has overshadowed our family has once and for all been shattered.

By Anonymous

I think because of my mental illness I've become a very accepting and nonjudgemental person. I have made many friends with mental illnesses too along the way and we have helped eachother to get through our difficult times. I met them at NAMI events, in the hospital, through cognitive therapy programs, in groups, and through volunteering. My fiance' has a mental illness as well. We met eachother at a support group almost eight years ago and we are still together and very supportive of each other even today. I am so happy to have him in my life and don't know what I would do if something happened to him. He is great. I am lucky to have so many family and friends who are so accepting of me despite my diagnosis. I am very grateful.

By NAMISD.1.5g

The condition has brought me in to new relationships and friendships by me attending the support group meeting thru NAMI. These are meetings for families who have siblings with any mental illness.

By Anonymous

How has the reality of the illness affected the way you engage and interact with others?

I try not to pass judgment when I see or drive by a homeless person on the street talking to himself, asking for money or dressed in dirty clothes. I always think that could be my brother wandering the streets, not knowing what to do or where to go and people being afraid of my brother hurting them and that's the reason people would not approach him to offer help. It's just because they don't know or understand that my brother or someone like my brother has a mental illness.

By grome_420

Do you feel mental illness has resulted in dependency relationships? If not, why not?

There are multiple facets to this: the caregiver begins to believe that all normal coping in the world depends upon their functions and thus coping with the illness defines the self, and thus the self becomes dependent on the illness. Further, the sick partner is often in such anguish that dependency on medications is a compassionate choice, even though a diminishing one. The relationship itself is dependent on 'coping', not thriving, or exploring or even just being.

By Anonymous

Is there anything else that has happened to you or that you've experienced in this area that you would like to share?

I would just like to say my life was in turmoil before the fact that sobriety, medicine, and good desicions and choices are saving me everyday.

By Anonymous

I wrote a poem for my son. I wanted him to know that he was special to me. I tried to show how he is, a handful and yet the joy of my life. The poem isn't the greatist but here it is: It is called MY TWO LEGGED MONSTER

I have a two legged monster that no one understands. Please let me explain so maybe you can.

My two legged monster was small and then he grew. I knew he was special since the active age of two.

He's quite tall now handsome and trim. But he still gets into trouble every now and then.

He's hardly ever grippy or sad and hardly gets mad. He's usually upbeat and pretty darn glad.

He has a positive nature and a really big smile. You can hear him laughing for almost a mile.

Everyone likes him, they want to take him home. But he's MY two legged monster and can't be left alone.

He's got lot of hobbies and and some raelly cool pets. Sometimes he's demanding and throws little fits.

He's a two legged terror but mostly a mischeift one. He likes to tease others, for him this is fun.

He has some pretty strange and some very jazzy friends. Some of them I like, the rest it depends.

I have a two legged monster and I love him so. One day I will have to let him go.

I cherish every moment with him even when I'm mad. He can put a smile on my face whenever I am sad.

I will always treasure my memories of him and his love. He knows I will always be there even when push comes to shove.

You see he's my two legged monster and I wouldn't change a thing. Because I know one day just for him the city's bells will ring!
By Anonymous

Things you learned

What do you think are the best ways to disclose the issues around mental illness to others?

I feel that it shouldn't be sugar coated. Be honest & explain it in laymans terms so that others may understand or relate to the situation in some way. It has been my experience that when I mention to people that my brother has Schizophrenia I get the deer in the headlights look, but when I start to tell them that he looks normal and they wouln't be able to tell until they have a conversation with my brother. That's when I see the other person change their facial expression or body language. I think they're just afraid of what they don't know or understand. I was like that too. The minute I herd the word Schizophrenia, I would think to myself, "ok, crazy", but now I understand that its not true. It's just an illness.

By grome_420

We did not say much to others. There was the feeling of hiding this. It was all going to go away. We told our son not to tell others. Not to tell employers, but I believe we read about this also. Sources had said to get the job and then maybe down the road, if necessary, tell your boss. This is a real Catch 22, but I know I read this which suggests even professionals know telling others that one is dealing with a mental illness can create a problem for the individual!

When I did get around to telling the people at the CCC he was working with, that he was acting out because of high anxiety, they would not believe me and gave me a deaf ear. Our son never did understand why he wasn't working with them anymore. (And this is a state organization to HELP young adults!!!)

I just don't know about disclosure. Perhaps if people with mental illness received the same aid as those with mental disabilities something would change. (We were so close at getting help and work for our son, but this county employee was not able to help because it was a mental "illness.")

By BC

How do you overcome barriers to communication – both with those who have a mental illness and with the people around them?

I overcome communication barriers by sharing my experiences as a sibling of a brother with Schizophrenia and making the person with mental illness feel confortable.
By Anonymous

How do you build intimacy with someone who has a mental illness?

I think it's actually easier to be intimate with someone with a mental illness if you have a diagnosis as well, like my fiance' and I. We both have Bipolar Disorder and I think that makes us a lot more understanding of each others struggles and issues. If one person has a mental illness and the other doesn't I think it's a lot more difficult to be intimate because there's a lot less personal understanding and acceptance. I think the best way though, regardless of diagnosis, is for both members of the couple to make sure the other doesn't feel alone, and for the couple to become educated about each others past life and illness. Basically, if you want to be intimate you must show you care.
By NAMISD.1.5g

First things first. Education about the particular mental illness is key. Unconditional love and understanding is key. In OCD (or any other illness), we're usually told by someone who isn't educated (about mental illness) to "just get over it", "you're overreacting" or even just a look that says "you're crazy." A lot of times, they're watching to see if you'll follow through with your compulsion.

In my experience, when someone close took the time to even try to understand the illness...it was the beginning to intimacy. Such a load off the shoulders! It's so hard for the OCD-er to understand what's happening and to feel support & love from another is a huge start on the road to some kind of recovery.

By Anonymous

What have been your biggest relationship challenges and how have you dealt with them?

The biggest relationship challenge that has arisen as a result of the impact of a diagnosis of mental illness in my family is dealing with the stigma that surely raises it ugly head. I am still amazed at the lack of compassion and understanding that exists around the illness....or perhaps it is just the discomfort in discussing it. From the early days of our family's diagnosis, our friends and own family members avoided the subject entirely, not that we opened any discussion with it. We had such a need to openly deal with our sorrow, frustration and loss of dreams for the vital life force of our son, but had nowhere to turn. We had co-occuring family diagnosis in both sides of our family, but any hopes to share ideas and questions were not welcomed. At every turn we accepted the realization we were silently on our own trying to cope and move through our lives.

Thankfully through NAMI, we learned how to carefully and quietly share information with those around us in a way that did not require any additional emotional effort. For example, before a recent extended family gathering, we simply sent an email to everyone that would be in attendance giving them a few facts about our son and why he could not be in attendance. This small step allowed us to avoid lengthy uncomfortable explanations for all concerned. We now realize a few well rehearsed comments to friends when asked about our son saves us grace and allows us to protect our son's privacy as well.

I am quite sure the biggest challenge has been my own fear and reluctance. Through NAMI I now realize mental illness is no different than any other chronic medical condition. Our son and family need support, love, and information as does any family supporting a loved one with such critical needs. I have learned to recognize those in my life that truly want to share our son's life and concerns and those that cannot bring themselves to discussion. I have watched our son realize the same conclusions. Once again the circle of friendships we all have found through NAMI support and sustain us.
By Anonymous

My biggest relationship challenges has been building patience. I have had to learn how to take a step back when I find myself frustrated and try to put myself in my brothers shoes to help myself understand someone with Schizophrenia.
By Anonymous

What impact has mental illness had on you and your family members? How has the illness affected your relationship?

The primary impact on me and on my children has been mistrust: we do not trust externals, we do not trust the professionals in the mental health arena, we do not trust other people except as their behavior over time warrants or earns that trust, and only slowly do we expose ourselves in any kind of relationship.
By Anonymous

I was an infant when my illness affected me. I had problems my whole life. Sometimes things would not bother me and other times they would make me blow up at my family. My parents and my brother got the worst of it. I would fight big time with them. Then I would feel awful. I knew I was in the wrong and I thought I won't blow up again, but it would happen a lot. I knew I was wrong but I couldn't stop it. I was teased by kids in school, and I took everything to heart. The kids would say mean things to me and made me feel like I was a rotten person. I was bullied a lot. I don't know why, but it happened the whole time I was in school. I hated school but I went and tried my best. I was nice to everyone but it didn't matter. I had one or two friends. That was all. Since the kids hated me I thought my family couldn't love me either. I guess I looked for proof that they couldn't possibly love me. I did that my whole life.

Well, I am 51 and one night I was crying and my son asked me what was wrong. I told him that I had tried to be a good mom, and a good daughter, but that I was just a big nothing. He said, Mom I know you try and so does everybody else in the family. They do love you. I didn't believe him but it made me feel better, then he said even when I am mad at you, you know I still love you right? I said yeah, so? He said well you know when you get mad at me, you still love me right? I said Yeah. He said, why do you think you aren't loved back? I said well, I don't think you all really love me. But he said that's just you. I am not sure when, but in the last month, I thought about that and I realized that yes! My family does love me, I mean really loves me. My mom really does love me!!!!

That was so important to me but I never really knew it. Now I do. Maybe it was my illness and maybe some of it was her, and maybe some of it was the hard lessons she was teaching me my whole life, but now I know she really does love me. Maybe it was it her culture, maybe I expected her to be like my friends' moms, but it doesn't matter anymore, because I know she loves me my illness and all that. I am sure if I weren't ill it would have been easier but I am ill, and I know she loves me even though I am different! All that matters to me is I know it now. I wouldn't trade my mom for anything in the world. I am glad that I know it, even though it took me 51 years to figure it out. Maybe I had to learn it the hard way so I wouldn't take it for granted. I am proud of my mom and now I have to make up for lost time and the best part is, I can do it. I tried to hate her so I could cope, but I was wrong to do that. Now, I just want to be the daughter she wanted and to make her happy and take care of her.

Life doesn't always give us what we want when we want, but it can give us what we need in time if we are patient, and that is hard to be sometimes when things are difficult. I am so glad that I know this now because I know I am really happy and that is a big part of being well. Maybe it's my medicine too. Maybe it was the hard work of my family, my doctor and my therapist. Maybe I just needed to open my heart and see that I wasn't such a bad person that the kids in school made me believe I was. I just know that my mental illness makes me me and that it makes my son him and that isn't bad, we have gifts that maybe other people don't have. Maybe it takes us time to figure things out, but I don't take anything for granted. My dreams are all coming true.
By Anonymous

It has brought us together, or closer, but it has also caused alot of disagreements among us as to who will care for my brother with Schizophrenia. I think there has been some recentment on my part beacuse I feel like I have always been the one talking with the doctors, nurses, psychiatrist, cops, paramedics, etc. and sometimes it can be overwhealming. I feel that on many occassions I had to be the strong one and keep my composure so that I could deal with some of the things that have happened with regards to my brother, and help in finding a resolution for whatever the situation is at that point in time. Sometimes I didn't alow myself to cry or was to busy fixing the problem. I didn't take time to deal with my own emotions. It has soften me up more, I cry when I see someone standing by a freeways entrace asking for money for food. I think about how that could have been my brother if it

147

wasn't that he is 100 % American disabled vet and has full VA benefits.

By grome_420

In a word - divisive. Truthfully, to this day I'm afraid to see my family becuase there are so many painful memories and experiences, so many fights and disagreements in the past that I literally get sick to my stomach just thinking about being around them. Sick or not, they have made choices about their lives that I don't agree with and don't want anything to do with. I feel constant pressure from my mother who is still alive to 'go along' and 'make nice' to keep the peace in the family when we're together. That's a worthwhile goal, but I'm not willing to do it at the expense of having my kids subjected to a barage of filth that flows from my sociopathic brother. I'd like to help him, but I can't change him and I can't make him abandon what I consider to be a socially, emotionally and morally bankrupt lifestyle.

If there is anything I've learned as a lesson in this whole thing, it is to be true to yourself. There will be times in a relationship (even a close family relationship like a brother) where you literally have to cut it off to protect your own soul. That's a very hard thing to do, but some people are truly toxic and they will drag you down with them if you let them. I think of it this way - if two people fall into a pit and one finds the way out he has a choice. He can either climb out and hope that he inspires or helps the other to do the same, or he can stay down in the pit to keep the other one company. The first choice offers hope. The second one is hopeless.

By Anonymous

Are there any other things that you have learned about this topic that you would like to share with us? What are we not asking you,

*that we should be asking you, if we knew to ask
it?*

Suicide is an Illness
When a person takes his own life, not only does he die in
body, but much of his spirit here on earth dies as well,
more so than for someone who had an "ordinary" death.

Why? Because nobody knows what to say, and there
seems to be no statute of limitations on silence. The
shame of suicide stiffens people's tongues, sometimes
permanently. Loved ones might fondly reminisce at
Christmas dinner about the grandmother who valiantly
fought cancer until the bitter end, but try that if the
family member died by his own hand. Chances are that
that topic will be met with a good deal of awkwardness
and discomfort. There is no valiance in losing to yourself.

With suicide, it is commonly believed that the cause of
death lies in the character of the person himself, his
inability to "appreciate what he has" or "cope" or "suck it
up." The individual who kills himself demonstrates
weakness in the worst way, taking the "easy way out." He
has no faith. He doesn't love his family enough. He gives
in. He gives up.

I do not accept this. I believe that individuals who commit
suicide have succumbed to a "toxin" (a.k.a. mental illness)
that first attacks the mind and eventually corrupts and
corrodes "the soul." The victims of suicide experience
psychic pain so intense that their powers of reason are
warped, their mental defenses compromised, and their
souls fractured. In this state, the "logical solution" to end
this level of suffering is for the person to end it himself.
I believe that individuals attacked by this caliber of
mental illness do not in fact kill "themselves." At this
point, the thing that we call the "true self" has ceased to
exist. The "self" is no longer separate from the predator
that has penetrated it and is ready to destroy it. The
individual who dies is simply doing the illness' dirty work.

149

I have seen this pattern too many times, and I would prefer not to see it again. I have known people, known well and loved well, that have suffered in this way and died horribly. Few talk about it. Few talk about it, not only because of the shame and the pain of loved ones associated with it, but because the ghastly nature of the deaths often overshadows the true quality of the lives they lived.

I am going to talk a bit about one of my friends now, T.Y., a man who I credit with keeping me afloat when I was at my lowest point in life. I met T.Y. in September, 1990, three months after the death of my father who passed away after a long struggle with bipolar depression.

T.Y. was one of my most beloved, cherished friends, my best friend at UCSD. He was an accomplished poet, scholar, and athlete. He drank copious amounts of coffee and loved to critique anything and everything. He graduated valedictorian of Muir College at UCSD in Classics and Philosophy and earned a full scholarship for the PhD program at Stanford. He could read Latin and Greek with the same fluency as English. He had sinister laugh and equally sinister personality. We took a great dislike to each other at first sight and then became even greater friends. Our favorite thing to do together was walk in the fog at night at UCSD under the neon sign of the Seven Vices and Seven Virtues, as the huge neon letters flashed on and off, turning the fog all the colors of the rainbow. T.Y. would often say that walking around the campus at UCSD was like walking inside of a glowing computer chip. To me, the nights spent walking around with T.Y. were among the best times of my life.

T.Y. passed away shortly after finishing his dissertation at Stanford, before his oral exams. He died of bipolar disorder with psychotic features. He was 27 years old.

It took me a long time to come to terms with the method of my father's and T.Y.'s deaths. They were both clearly mentally ill at the time they took their own lives, and yet

I still felt abandoned. I blamed them in my heart, even though intellectually I knew that they suffered from something greater than themselves. It has only been with time that I came to realize that depression is a "thing," like a virus, and potentially lethal.

I no longer blame my loved ones. I evoke my father's name at family gatherings—his love of the USC Trojans, for example, and at times, you will even hear me reciting T.Y.'s poetry.
By NAMISD.1.6h

Siblings

Things that happened

When and how did the behaviors of your brother or sister seem different, or cause you problems?

I remember the day that my parents brought my baby brother home from the hospital. At 4 years old, I thought this new little bundle of joy was brought home specifically for me and would become my favorite toy and in many ways he did. However that first night, when I was full of energy, he, unfortunately, was not! Over the years my brother became my friend, my collaborator, my partner in crime. While the 4 year age difference did get in the way at times, for the most part, we maintained a close relationship. I am sure there were moments that my brother thought I was being a little to bossy, but what older sibling hasn't been accused of that one!

The first time I noticed that something seemed different was when we had moved to San Diego. It wasn't that he had a hard time handling change, in fact, it was just the opposite. He was an excited 7 year-old that had new creeks to discover and friends to make. He had a new bike, that was made for an adult, but he didn't care. (That was the daredevil in him.) At this same time that he was exploring his new surroundings, he also started to worry. He worried about things a 7 year-old shouldn't even really be aware of and these worries turned into anxiety. After about a year, he seemed to be able to manage his anxiety, or hide it, though you could still tell that certain things would cause him to worry. For example, he could never leave the house without saying, 'I love you' to my parents.

It wasn't until his senior year in high school that a more serious disorder was emerging. By this time, I had moved out of the house and was in my final year of college. Over the years since his diagnosis, I have questioned would it have made a difference if I had remained living at my parents? I know I couldn't have known that life for my brother was going to get hard, but even today, I feel guilty for abandoning him. I will never forget this one conversation with him that confirmed to me something was up. We were sitting in my parent's car while they had gone into the grocery store and he started to talk to me about God. Which at first doesn't sound unusual, especially since we had just come from church, unless you heard the rest of the conversation. He could tell that I was getting uncomfortable and concerned and therefore decided to change the subject.

This was the first of many unique conversations about God. My family and I still weren't quite able to put our finger on what might be challenging my brother, so like so many other families we turned to the possibility of drug and alcohol abuse. While this was an issue for him, it was through this path that we discovered his underlying illness. And like so many other families, this started us on a roller coaster of a journey.

By Anonymous

My sister has Paranoid Schizophrenia. Most of the time she refuses to admit that she has the disease. When she is taking her medication like she is supposed to, she knows and understands that she has a problem. But like so many people, when she starts feeling better, she stops taking her medication because she doesn't feel like she needs it anymore.

Her paranoia started simply. Sometimes we would go to the store shopping and she would hear someone start laughing. She was absolutely sure they were laughing at her and she would get furious. Then it got so that she was unable to keep a job because she thought that all of her coworkers were against her and out to sabotoge her.

She regularly calls family members and fights with them about things that happened many years ago. This has gotten worse over time.

Now she has progressed to barely leaving the house because of her various paranoias which include fear of catching a terrible virus like bird flu or getting into a wreck and her insurance not covering it.
By J44489

When was the term mental illness first mentioned and by whom? Who tried to explain things to you?

I first heard about my brother Michael's mental illness when he was involuntarily taken into county general by PERT. He had been acting different for about two years before we as a family finally had him committed to the mental health unit at San Diego County Mental. Michael had paranoid thoughts and voices and this caused him to look completely vacant from the outside. His face seemed to show that his mind was very far away from the conversation you were having with him. The therapist at county mental was the first person to diagnose Michael, and it was the first time we had heard of his mental illness. My first response was, "Michael doesn't have multipule personalities?" which was a myth associated with Schizophrenia. I soon learned what the definition of "schizophrenic" was.
By Anonymous

Well, my mom and dad knew when they adopted me that I was going to have problems. When I was growing up I wasn't very smart. My parents told me I was sensitive.

They never told me I was ill. I think they didn't want any limits put on me. My dad was a social worker and he kept me busy. My folks would sit up at night with me and to teach me math, they used lots of coins and when I got the answers right, they let me keep the coins and I could buy anything I wanted. They also took me to many trips so I could see and hear about history. I wasn't too good about learning so they found really great ways to teach me things and so I could keep up with the other kids at school. When I was in junior high, they got me a tutor to help me. They made the tutor teach me and they made sure she also listened to me talk too. She was very nice.

My folks also made sure I saw counselors my whole life, so for me it was normal and I just thought everyone saw them. I think at some point when I was in my 20's my psychiatrist and I talked about my illness. He explained it to me in a very nice way. He took the approach like my dad would have. That was when I also first tried medicine. My dad would sometimes tell me I was naive but he never put me down. I was really naive and I was used by a lot of kids, but one day I learned about all that stuff.

Now I feel better. I do not feel bad about my illness because now after all these years, I undertand it and I can use the good parts of it to help me. I know my parents loved me a lot because I was hard to live with. I know I made their lives a living hell, and I think they knew I was going through my own private hell too. I feel very fortunate that I had the mom and dad I had.

After I found out I was ill, my dad was very supportive of me and he would send me articles to help me and my son. He also would listen to me and give me good advice. My psychiatrist also is real suppportive too. He tells me when he thinks I am doing a good job, just like my dad, he is proud of me too.

I can be myself and I can let my illness out of me when no one is around because I can control it better now. What I mean is I can make my funny faces at night when no one is here. I can also make my little dance things that I only do in private. I can make my little steps and dance around like an elf or a make believe fairy. I like that because it is fun. My brother and I talk about illness and even though it is hard for him, he really tries to understand it and he is doing a good job sometimes at it.

By Anonymous

What impact did their illness have on you and your family? How did you feel about the ways their illness impacted your life?

Pretty negative and very destructive. Watching the nightmare unfold for my parents I tried to be the 'good kid' and to compensate for my brother's destructive behavior by being as constructive as I could be. I focused on school and did very well. I stayed quiet, stayed out of the way and internalized everything to the point that I developed a bleeding ulcer. I think it was only after I spent a few days in the hospital at 13 that my parents even thought about what the entire 'scene' at home was doing to me.

In regards to how I felt about the ways this impacted my life - I hated it and I hated him because of it. I think the best way to describe the feeling of that period of my life is like being trapped in a mine shaft a mile underground. Imagine having no light, no way to find a light, no idea of how to get out of the mine or of which direction to turn, and the CERTAIN knowledge that any move you make might set off another cave in that could kill you. It makes me sick 35 years later just to think about it.

I got especially angry at the time because I thought all of my brother's behavior was a choice to be an arrogant, self-center, lying little SOB. I laid a large measure of the blame for my parents divorce on him. That's probably unfair, but I'm sure the stress he brought to their marriage didn't help at all. I never understood that he was really ill. To this day I don't know how much control he really had over his behavior. And sadly, even though I can now intellectualize the fact that he has a physical issue that impacts the way he is, I still have a very hard time forgiving him and it's very difficult for me to be in the same room with him. I have to move past those feelings and forgive, but it's hard for me to do that. I really have to work at it and that's a very embarrassing, depressing admission to make.

By NAMISD.1.1a

Things you learned

How have you managed to stay close to your sibling through the depths of their illness?

Michael and I are only four years apart in age so part of staying close was to involve both of our groups of friends. Since Michael started developing his mental illness in college, his friends had met me before and it was very easy to stay in touch. Many of my close friends have also been like siblings to Michael and wanted to be a support system for me and my family. Since we have so many friends and family members that want Michael to go through a healthy recovery they want to show they care. NAMI San Diego has given them an outlet to stay involved. The NAMI Walk has given me the opportunity to talk more about mental illness, and our family's experience with it. Through having a team in the NAMI Walk every year our family has been able to bring awareness, strength and education to everyone that knows our family. Michael also makes an effort to stay close to our family. He tries to come over to my mom's house and just be around for us to love him. He makes an effort to read stories to his nephews and always tries to let us know how he is feeling. Michael understands that he has a mental illness, and understands how difficult his struggles are for everyone to understand. He takes the time to answer our questions, instead of getting mad or frustrated, and this makes us feel more comfortable. Michael chooses to stay involved in our family and that is just as important as his family wanting him to recover well.

By NAMISD.1.3j

What is the most important thing you've learned about having a brother or sister with mental illness?

The most important thing I have learned from having a sister who is mentally ill is patience. I have to be patient with her and understand that she has a mental problem that she has very little control over.

I have to understand that the terrible things she says are not right or reasonable. What she says when she is in one of her "down" times is not who I believe she really is. When she calls me ready to fight about something that happened 20 years ago, I just have to be patient and not get angry right back.

I have come to realize that I will probably have to take care of my sister on a full time basis some day. As she grows older (she is now 32), her mental problems grow worse. For now, she is able to live on her own. But I know that someday I will have to step in and make some tough decisions for her own good.

By J44489

Are there any other things that you have learned about this topic that you would like to share with us? What are we not asking you, that we should be asking you, if we knew to ask it?

My brother is a "Normie" but I think I am better adjusted then him in some respects, because I see a therapist and he doesn't. Anyway, when I found out my son was ill I felt like it was my fault. I was ill and I passed this onto my kid. But you know what? I can understand him and be here for him. I love him just the way he is because even though he can be awful, he has his loving side too. I think it is important he shares his thoughts with me and he does, he trusts me with whatever is going on in his mind. I also know that he cares about some things and that even though he has problems he is ok.

My brother doesn't understand some things about mental illness but sometimes he makes an effort. My sibling, my brother isn't ill, so I can tell you this, sometimes he thinks my intuition is out there, but it really isn't. Sometimes he gets surprised.

My child is very hard to deal with sometimes, such as his way of being insistent on who he believes he is from day to day, but it keeps me on my toes! I once told my dad I didn't want a normal everyday boring life. He said becareful what you wish for, you might get it.

Well, I don't have normal! I have an interesting life and it certaintly keeps me going. I don't always agree with my son, but we are doing much better now. He didn't want to take medication for a long time, then when he was in the hospital, my mom and I said, well, if you don't want to be in the hospital take the medicine unless you like being away from home then don't take it. Now he gets shots and is doing better.

I think it is important to never give up. My family didn't give up on me and now I am doing ok. Sometimes it takes a while to feel comfortable with yourself, but you will. Don't give up on yourself, you can do it and it doesn't have to be done in one day either. Give yourself lots of time to grow and give yourself a chance to make mistakes and then be good to yourself for trying and be proud that you are you. Give yourself a chance to become a friend to someone, a spouse, or even a student. Give yourself a chance to become an older wiser person with a lifetime of memories to share.

By Anonymous

When Parents have a Mental Illness

Things that happened

When and how did the behaviors of your parent seem different, or cause you problems?

My mother began displaying, "signs" of a mental illness about 10 years ago. At that time she was 49 years old. At the time I did not know the severity of it or what was going on. I lived six hours away. My mother and father were also married at the time and my father for his own reasons did not tell me when it suddenly starting happening. After a few months my father began to tell me that my mom was seeing things, hearing things, and she was fearful that people were following her.
By Anonymous

There was always a family history that we knew, but did not appreciate. My grandfather (father's father) was bi-polar and committed suicide in 1935 when my father and his two brothers were young boys. My father grew up and went to college and then law school. He joined the military, became a JAG officer and eventually rose to the rank of Colonel in the Marine Corps. One of his brothers went to divinity school and became a pastor. The brother who became a pastor developed Schizophrenia and went through a series of electro-shock treatments in the late 1950's. He died in a car accident, but there was some question as to whether he had crashed the car on purpose.

When I was 14 my father deployed to Vietnam. I don't know if he ever saw combat; that was kept from me. After 13 months he returned, but the man I knew as my father never came home. He had totally changed. My father was gone and in his place was this new man. It was bizarre. The man that came home was a stranger to me. It was horrifying. The man who returned was unrecognizable. He was in a manic state when he came back; he was in a very high manic episode. It was very earth-shattering. We were expecting Daddy and we got this very bizarre strange thing. To have a stranger living under your roof with you who is this foul minded, smoking, abusive, person saying things and doing things they had never done before and just acting bizarrely is very frightening for a young girl. He started cheating on my mother and drinking heavily. My mother was just torn apart.

My brother and I were fearful, scared, mystified. We weren't allowed to talk about emotional issues or ask questions. We were supposed to focus on school and get straight A's and ignore the elephant's tap dancing in the living room wearing purple polkadot tutus. We were expected to go on to college and put on a good show, to buck it up, get out there and dance the tune, be responsible and do your duty.

My parents split up and my father deteriorated. When it became apparent that something was very wrong my father was scheduled to have electroconvulsive therapy or electroconvulsive shock therapy ("ECT"), but because of what his brother had been through he was terrified of it. The day before he was scheduled to start ECT he laid down in front of the back wheels of a semi-truck that pulled away from the curb and ran over him and crushed him to death.

Looking back on it my mother believes that Daddy was bi-polar from the time that they were married, but that condition was undiagnosed in those days and people just didn't talk about it.
By Anonymous

I didn't realize my mother was different- she was just

162

mom...she was moody. Way up excited- really fun to be with- cooking and baking in huge quanties, etc. or in bed.

I really didn't realize she had Bi-Polar until I was diagnosed and recognized the symptoms. Her undiagnosed untreated depression killed her. She shot herself at age 50- I was 30 yrs. old. My father didn't exhibit symmptoms until his late 70's. We just thought he complained a lot. He killed himself at age 79.
By Anonymous

My father's behaviors weren't a drastic change from one day to the next. At some point we knew that things were getting worse and we started connecting the dots that he might have depression. It started slow. He began not wanting to visit my brother and sister, began resenting me for small comments or suggestions I would make. As his depression got worse, he would isolate himself from the family and no longer attended any family events. We couldn't drag him out of his room, no matter what we did to try to convince him. Until at his lowest point of his depression he started giving away his things to his grandchildren. At first it was yellow flags that had us thinking, and then they became drastic red flags.
By Anonymous

What did you notice? What caused you to wonder why they behaved the way they did?

I was able to see it first-hand when my mother and father came to visit me in San Diego. We went to Anthony's on Pacific Coast Hwy. and we ordered shrimp cocktail. I ordered our food and brought our trays to our table. My mother stared at her food and then she stared at mine. She said, "Why don't we switch." it was such a distrusting tone. It literally crushed me. I was 27 at the time, but I still felt like a little girl getting her heart broken for the

very first time. I was angry inside. I said to myself, "Why doesn't she trust me??" During this particular time it was already 4-5 months after she began behaving this way. She was always accusing my father of trying to poison her. She would throw food away in the refrigerator. She thought people were constantly following her and she would refer to them as, "The Posse." However, I did not have a true grasp of it all until this very poignant moment when she refused to eat food set forth before her, which was from her own daughter. It broke my heart.
By Anonymous

When was the term mental illness first mentioned and by whom? Who tried to explain things to you?

My mother was not, has not been diagnosed. The family practitioner whom she saw for 10 years under regular/general circumstances discharged her around the same time she began to become paranoid, confrontational, and delusional. However, it did not take a rocket scientist to see that she was displaying signs of a mental illness. Additionally she also has siblings who are diagnosed schizophrenic, bipolar, and/or with depression. Therefore, it was not hard to see what was occurring.
By Anonymous

I never heard the term Mental Illness until I came to NAMI. Even my Psychiatrists only said Depression or Bi-Polar. When I took the In Our Own Voice training and I heard I had a brain disorder, an illness like any other, it was such a relief.
By NAMISD.1.4c

164

What impact did this illness have on you and your family?

Hind sight is really 20/20 as is education. When you are young and move on, trying to create your own, you do not realize how family events can or have impacted you, your life, your childrens' life, your siblings life or your relationship with them. Even in a family full of love and support, there is apparently lingering stories/stuff.

I am the 1st born of 4 children. Our mother became "sick" when I was in 6th grade. I took it as my responsibility to care for the other 3 kids, cook dinners, laundy, homework, etc after our mother had so many shock treatments she did not remember she had any kids. To put that in perspective, the time frame is early to mid 70's. They treat "consumers" differently now.

Long story short, I became an emancipated minor at 15. I became pregnant at 17 and chose to keep the baby by myself and said no to marriage. It is now 35 years later and I do not regret any of those decisions. Yet, life was difficult and had and has continued to show its face because of our life events. I was so young and even though I felt independent and strong and ready to go, I have since seen and still see how this, really, was (is) not true. To date, I am the only person I know that was an "emancipated minor." My doing so was years before that movie "Irreconcilable Differences." My life has been "backward"; i.e. I did things in reverse of what "the social norm and probably healthy way of doing things was." First, I had the baby, then bought a house, then married (my son was 11), and then college. Nothing was easy. I had no family by me. My parents divorced before my child was two; my mother moved out of state with two siblings and my father moved on. I was alone, by choice and by circumstance. My father, God Bless his soul, is still with us to date. I hope I have his genes!

My son, is incredible. I became a designated and accomplished professional. Both my son and I contribute a lot to our fellow man. To my pain, he has called himself "a bastard" years ago because I was not married. If I could take it away, I would; but I cannot, any more than what happened to me. My siblings also have done well, but not without their own pain, One of them was and is, but still trying not to, be angry at me for leaving decades ago. Time does not heal all wounds; it is what you do with that that time that counts. The youngest sibling, who knew their Mother the least before she became sick, and who is 7 years my junior, shows their pain in a different way. All 4 kids finally found their way, but life has never been like society said. We were all behind the "8 ball", but given enough love by our parents when we were young to all to be able to move on with Christ, with family, with each other, with hope.

By NAMISD.1.5h

It caused me to go into great fear experiencing alarm and serious apprehension. My father was gone and a stranger had taken his place. I didn't know this new man with a new personality; new moods; new expectations; new judgments; new concerns; thoughts; new emotions. It was very unsettling. The onset of my own illness occurred shortly thereafter.

As an alcoholic, severe Bipolar 1 in the 1970's and early 1980's with only old mood stabilizers and old anti-depressants, his illness was not well managed by the military. His illness only brought tension, grief, stress, pressure, worry, and anxiety into my life. He left my mother for numerous other women, spent their life savings, lived a chaotic and turbulent life in and out of hospitals, gave away his life insurance policy and then committed suicide.

By Anonymous

*Is there anything else that has happened to you
or that you've experienced in this area that you
would like to share?*

After my parents committed suicide there was anger
shame and guilt. I've learned that they had a mental
Ilness and they didn't see a choice. I'm not to blame- nor
is anyone else. They are not cowards, they did not do it to
punish.

In the same vent, I am not a bad person. I have an illness
like any other. I have a brain disorder and treatment,
coping strategies and my spirituality help me stay in
Recovery. I live the best day each day I can and I advocate
for others by telling my story.

I tell my parents' story on a DVD NAMI San Diego made
in conjunction with San Diego County Mental Health,
Aging Independent Service and University of California
San Diego Geriopsych Department entilted "Not Just the
Blues."
By Anonymous

Things you learned

*If you felt like the illness 'took them away', how
did you deal with the sense of loss?*

I don't think I ever have gotten over the sense of loss, but
I've learned to deal with it. I always wanted a parent I
could talk to, reason with, work through problems with. I
craved a parent that I could go to for intelligent counsel
and guidance, but that wasn't in the cards. The loss hurts,
but I'm probably a stronger person for it.
By Anonymous

I haven't really dealt with the loss of my mother. I am very resentful and angry. I think to myself, "All you have to do is take a pill!!!" Yet, she does not think there is anything wrong with her. I truly understand what she is experiencing is truly her reality. At the same time there are those moments in between her bad days when she is my mom. She is,"normal." She is the mom I KNOW, love, and miss more than anything. And so, I think, "WHY??? Why won't you get help!!!" It breaks my heart to see her the way she is. It is almost 10 years later

By Anonymous

When my mother was depressed she got migranes a lot and would stay in bed with room dark. We had to stay really quiet.

When she was manic, she'd get me up in the middle of the night to watch a favorite movie or dance around the living room. She was really happy then.

My father would come home from work, sit in his recliner and go to sleep.

I wished we could have dinner together and go places like my friends.

By NAMISD.1.4c

Who or what have been the best resources to help you deal with a parent with mental illness, and what have they done to help you?

NAMI and in particular, the Family to Family program, was the best resource for me.

I knew my mom was "sick" but did not really understand. I was an adult in my 40's, and had not been "around it" until she had a relapse. We were all together to celebrate a rare Christmas together as a full family. Me, my son, my siblings, my nephew all cried and tried to understand. The behavior was devastating for us all. She would not take a shower because she thought their were cameras in the vents. She would not eat because she thought we were trying to poison her. We could not get her out of bed for days. She was depressed but also verbally ugly/mean.

I went back to Texas and sought EAP, Employee Assistance Counseling. I asked for someone that specialized in bi-polar to help me understand my Mother. I went to the suggested therpaist who suggested I go to a bi-polar support group; A friend, Ellen, asked if I wanted company; I told her I did not know why, but said sure. We went and then found out it was a suppport group for those with bi-polar. That facilitator told me/us about the Family to Family program. I went to that program by myself, but was fine and found it life changing.

Bottom Line? The Family to Family program changed all of our lives for the better. I was afraid of public speaking, just like most, but after my FTF course, I became a FTF teacher, trained in Austin and taught more than one course. From a professional standpoint, I then became involved in Toastmasters. From a personal perspective, NAMI and the FTF program changed our life. They gave me the education, tools, understanding, and support to better care for my mother and for myself. My mother opened up to me more than she ever had because she was proud of me for taking those classes, becoming a teacher, and helping other families and consumers. She thought I understood and she was right, I did because of what I learned from you and others involved in simlar life situations. I became a mental health advocate and some of my friends became advocates as well because of the knowledge I shared with them.

Life would have been so much easier if I knew about you earlier. I will always be an adocate because of what you

did for me, my mother, my family and my friends. Thank you NAMI!
By NAMISD.1.5h

For me support groups have never been the best source of support. Although quite important for many people, I have never been able to sit through an entire support group. But, I knew about the free 12 week course Family-to-Family through NAMI San Diego and decided to take the time out of my busy schedule to take the class. I had put it off for so long because I had to work and keep my own sanity by taking time for myself, no matter how stressful the situation had gotten with my father. He continued to refuse treatment and at that time I was going through my own anger phase. Deciding: "oh well, it's up to him, I've tried my best." But I couldn't completely give up on him.

I finally put a pause to my busy life and quickly realized that the reasons why I had put off taking the class were all of a sudden no longer important. I thought: "Really? I could have known THIS long ago!" Could have, Should Have, Would Have, But Didn't. No matter at what time I took the class though, it was the best thing ever. Each class was jam packed with information and I was picking up things like a sponge. It gave me a different perspective on what he was going through and different ways to approach him.

Best thing that could have ever happened to me - and to him, for I was better at advocating for him after that.
By Anonymous

Care-Giving

Things that happened

What is the most important thing you do in this role?

I volunteer at a local hospital. I work with people of all ages. I love what I do even though it isn't a lot. It is and it isn't. For me it's such a joy to be where I am that I really enjoy what I do. I help people out with what they need, mostly someone to talk to or share with. I like that because I can be me and it is ok. The people I help are like family so I always like to see them. I think they like that I can really understand them because we have our illness in common. The other thing I like is the co-workers I have also respect me. They treat me really nice and if I am not sure what someone needs I can get help and they still appreciate me.

I think it is important to be yourself and not put on airs or pretend to be someone you're not. I can tell when someone is not being honest with me and so can my "guys" so I always be honest with them and if I haven't the experience to understand their concerns I tell them that and they explain to me what they think so I can help someone else to get through their troubles.

I think the most important thing I do is listen and support them no matter what I feel. I also give lots of hugs. I get hugs too, which make me feel really good. I try to understand what a person feels and why they feel that way. I think it is important not to just hear words but to really listen, don't think of an answer or response until they are done talking because you will miss what they are saying. I think sometimes people think they know what a person is saying, but if your really listen and wait, you

171

might be surprised by what you can learn. I love to listen to people and talk with them, I call them 'my guys" because I really do care about them and I see them as people I really respect and just feel that they are teaching me as much as I am giving them. I think that is the best thing in the world.
By Anonymous

The most important thing I do in the caregiver role is to reframe it for myself, my daughter, and my helpful friends. My daughter is working on her recovery therefore I am a "recovery facilitator." For us, healthy dependency is not an acceptable goal. We both want her to be independent and to feel that she is making significant contributions to her world.

Just calling yourself a caregiver makes your shoulders droop. You are responsible for another human being and there is no end in sight. That is different from being the parent of a six year old that you expect to achieve independence by at least age 25. It leads to bitterness on the caregiver's part and resentfulness on the recipient's part.

If both people focus on the individual's recovery and can agree on what each needs to do to make that recovery a reality, it is seen as shared word rather than a burden for either.

I just wish that I had realized this long ago.
By 1curtis1

What changes did you have to make in your habits, lifestyle, schedule and expectations as a result of the mental illness?

Our lifestyle abruptly changed when our son was hit with mental illness. My wife and I went part time so one of us could be available 24/7. Our life centered on our son, with heightened anxiety and worry and confusion as to what to do everythig was forgotten other than what to do to get our son well. I did discover that during stressfull times it was most helpful to stay calm keep voice low and hold on to emotions and our son was able to function much better when he was going through a tough time.

By drive1

Things you learned

How have you dealt with the dependencies, time constraints, and resentments confronting a caregiver?

Sometimes the only way to preserve my own sanity has been to demand a separation from the situation. Demand isn't really the right word because it's not so much that I asked to withdraw from the care-giving relationship when it became suffocating, it's more like I finally resolved in my own mind to take a breath so I could stay alive. I guess the person of whom I demanded a change in care-giving behavior was me.

A little background would help. It sounds noble to selflessly give yourself away in the service of another day after day, month after month, year after year. Unfortunately, I haven't been able to do that without becoming very bitter, depressed and hopeless, and it has taken me a long time to come to grips with why I feel this way. I've struggled with this issue a lot and have come to the conclusion that it really is okay and great to take care of someone who really needs it. I have been in that position and have not resented it. I wanted to help and was glad to be able to do it. But there have been other times, in my first care-giving role where I have come to

173

realize that I was manipulated into caring for someone who was capable of caring for themselves but was either afraid to, didn't want to, or required constant acts of care as validations of the fact that someone loved them. In retrospect I think my problem was more one of care-giver exploitation and insufficient boundaries than anything else.

Whatever the cause the effect was that I felt completely drained of all my reserves to the point where I had nothing left and my own mental health became suspect. When I was much younger I contemplated suicide because my life had become enslaved to the incessant, psychotic demands of the person I cared for. I had to wait on this person hand and foot. I had to constantly do things for them that they were perfectly capable of doing for themselves, but they had me do them as proof of my affection. The problem was that provision of such proof was never sufficient and was required several times an hour no matter what else was going on. Whatever I was doing was inconsequential; my care-receiver thought absolutely nothing of interrupting me at any time when the need for validation moved them. There were no boundaries between us. In their mind I was an extension of them. I didn't exist as my own person. I didn't think I could ever escape. I was controlled by my care-receiver. I thought I owed them my total loyalty. I thought that this was the way things were for everyone - that this situation was normal. It was only after I started to get older and started to rebel that I began to see how dysfunctional this situation was. The problem that arose next was that my care-receiver went to great theatrics to compel my continued devotion. Like a little child throwing a tantrum to get what they wanted, I became the recipient of hysterical attempts to keep me in line. The more I withdrew, the more manic and outrageous the overtures became. In reality I was a drug that they needed and the withdrawal and detox was difficult.

I developed great resentment towards this person. But that has softened over time as I have come to understand

174

the nature of their mental illness. It's not that they don't care about me or my needs; it's that they are mentally incapable of putting themselves in the shoes of any other person. One of the saddest parts of this story for me is that the person I cared for has no appreciation of how much they asked of the people around them. I think one of the great challenges of mental illness, at least in my experience, is that it becomes an all consuming reality for the person with the condition. It's not that they become self-centered so much as they become completely self-absorbed. There is so much going on in their own head that they can't see anything outside of themselves or think about how what they are doing is impacting anyone else. It's as if their radar is turned off. They can't pick up any signals from the outside and they get to the point where they act like the outside doesn't even exist.

It's very hard to confess this publicly, even anonymously. I still question myself daily and constantly doubt whether I'm doing the right thing.

By Anonymous

What is your most important tool as a caregiver?

Giving of myself and time. I like to get to know people, I like to sit and talk. I love to listen and I love to hear answers to my questions. I really like to be where I am at, but, I also have to rest throughout the day. So I am going to work on making myself able to stay longer with people and do more. I think I have to say patience is a very important tool along with compassion. Oh and being yourself is very important. You have to feel comfortable or you just can't help another person because you won't be happy. I think sometimes we are here to help eachother and sometimes we are here to learn from eachother. But I think the best tool is love and to really care, then the rest just comes natural.

By Anonymous

What or who is your most important support and what makes it (or them) special?

My most important support is my NAMI family. It was from this group that I first learned about setting healthy and reasonable boundaries and that my daughter's bipolar disorder and substance abuse were not my fault and they were not her fault. Fifteen years later, NAMI folks still sustain me. They understand and share my anxieties and my daughter's triumphs without my having to give long explanations. In short, they listen well. They say the things that let me know that I'm understood. And, if I really want it, they help me problem solve. I am persuaded that NAMI saved my daughter's life and my emotional health.
By 1curtis1

What do you think is the most important lesson you can share about caring for someone with mental illness?

I am going to write this as speaking to myself...and my son...

I love my son. He has an illness, but the illness is no different than if he had diabetes. Encourage him to not identify himself as the illness.

Rather, focus on your dreams, your desires, what you want to be. We all have to do the same. Some things we can do, and some we cannot. That's okay!

Your life matters! You are a wonderful person and I love you, always!
By BC

Caring for mentally ill, in my opinion, takes an

176

extraordinary amount of patience and complete awareness of the need for compassion.

When feeling stress, take a time-out. Live one minute at a time not one day at a time. Enjoy the minute of peace and of being with your loved one.

Watch for any signs of problems associated with medications and do not hesitate to go with your "gut" feelings.

Get second, third, fourth opinions and don't fall for the doctor is always right opinion that permeates in our society... Be your own and your loved ones vigilant advocate..

Contact NAMI

Find whatever it is that will help you cope with the anxiety/stress: prayer, meditation, a sport, book.

For me, it was putting my son in the car and driving up and down the coast, he loved it also..
By drive1

To give your loved ones the opportunity to experience living as "normal" as they can. By treating and communicating with them in an honest and "normal" way and not treating them as if they are sick. To take care of yourself physically and emotionally. Going to support groups with NAMI. To keep them busy. To never give up. And, last but not least, to pray.

My daughter was diagnosed as Schizophrenic at the age of 17 going on 18. That was 28 years ago. She is now diagnosed as Schizoaffective. I did not know about this disease when she was first diagnosed in 1980 and did not know about NAMI until about 2-3 years into her illness. Maybe NAMI did not exist in back then, I don't know. I was at the mercy of the psychiatrists who really didn't know much about this disease either. In 1989, at one of my meetings at NAMI, there was a guest speaker, Dr. T. who had a sister with Schizophrenia and had written a book, "Surviving Schizophrenia", which I bought. I remember he had mentioned that Schizophrenics do better not living at home. That's when I began taking my chances with having my daughter experience life on her own, little by little, step by step.

I suggested that she live in her own apartment. She protested, saying "you are kicking me out into the world." I remember saying that it was because I loved her that I wanted her to live on her own. I took a big chance andI co-signed on her first apartment. She has lived on her own for approximately the last 20 yrs. She lived in public housing under the San Diego Housing Commission the last 15 years and is now on Section 8 as of last year. To be on Section 8 can take up to 5 years on the waiting list. But I believe, and don't quote me, that they give preferences to people with disabilities. There have been many "ups and downs" that naturally come with this disease. And sometimes, I have even questioned whether she should be living on her own, but I believe that she is happier. She has often told me she could never live with me and loves living on her own.

After she began successfully living on her own, I asked her if she wanted to work. She did and that's when I started the ball rolling again. Taking my chances that she could work. The State Department of Rehabilitation wouldn't take her case and her psychiatrists told me she could never work. I told my daughter if she wanted to work, she will. Having worked with the Employment Development Department, I knew what working did to people's self-esteem and I wanted that for my daughter. It was a struggle with the Department of Rehabilitation, but I kept "bugging" them. Finally, they took her case. She had a "job coach" and worked as a cashier for two years and had other jobs for another 2 years.

Then, she decided she was going to school. This has been the most positive event in her life, in my opinion. She enrolled herself at her community college and has been going to school the last two years. She, somehow, knew to sign up with the department that assists people with disabilities. She was on the Dean's List last year. However, these last couple of months have been hard on her and, I guess, with the pressure of finals, etc, etc. she had a breakdown. But now she is wanting to start going to school again. She will be going for her AA degree and has asked me to pray for her...so what do you think I will be doing? Supporting and encouraging her and, of course, keep praying.

By mamcita

Learning, Growth and Advocacy

Things that happened

What are your biggest regrets dealing with mental illness?

Seeking advice and acceptance from those who are incapable or unwilling of giving it. I can sing my "song" a thousand times, but if they don't like it, or can't understand it, they just won't listen. But someone else will embrace your "song" and you. They will most likely have a more trained and sensitive ear....with no ear plugs!
By Anonymous

One word: Embarrassment. I will never forget the first time I was embarrassed that my brother had a mental illness. We had just been informed about which illness he was struggling with, though the illness itself I was never really embarrassed by but more the symptoms expressed, and I wanted to take him out to lunch to allow my parents some respite and to grieve for the loss of the dreams they had for him. My husband and brother-in-law went with us. The whole way to the restaurant and at the restaurant, every now and then my brother would start laughing for absolutely no reason. There was nothing I could do or say to stop him from laughing and I felt uncomfortable because he wasn't conforming to society's rules on when one should laugh. I have looked back on this day and how I felt several times. And while I know that it is natural to be uncomfortable when placed in a situation that isn't quite what you expected, I never again felt that same embarrassment. In fact, every time since then when he would laugh for no reason that I was aware

of, I would ask him to share the story he was re-living that made him laugh so that I could join in on the laughter. Sure enough, many times he had some elaborate story that would make you laugh, and those moments where he didn't have a story, at the very least I knew he was happy and that is something to wish for everyone.
By NAMISD.1.1f

What are your proudest moments dealing with mental illness?

I have two areas I take pride in. One is taking charge helping in my son's defense. I feel as if I failed to do the right things before the world changed but I needed the courts to recognize the truth of the situation. Yes a horrific crime was committed but that it was the illness that caused it and it was not the nature of my son. Prison was not the answer to his insanity but that he needed mental heath services in the proper secure institution.

Secondly, I have been deeply involved in NAMI for the last 6 years and I am always pleased to be able to use these tragic circumstances and the knowledge I have accumulated since, to help other families who are really struggling.
By NAMISD.1.1b

The fact that after two bouts of serious depression in the early 90s, I went on to find new jobs and fulfill my profession and retire from there. I have been able to live a full life. And I think the fact that I faced the illness and myself and decided to deal with it.
By NAMISD.1.4i

I think my proudest moment was after my illness was used against me, not right away, but later. I felt like I didn't belong anywhere or with anyone. Then one day I found with the help of my psychiatrist and therapist that I have good feelings that lots of people over look. I care about people. I have sympathy and compassion for others. Maybe it comes from my own self. Maybe the way others treated me in bad ways gave me the ability to understand others better. I think one of my proudest moments was when I wrote to Governor Davis and he wrote back to me. I needed his help and had never written to an elected official except my dad. So I wrote to the Governor and asked for his help. He wrote back and I thought he wrote to everyone but he didn't. I got probably a dozen letters from him about this problem and he didn't think I was kookoo; well at least he looked into the problem and fixed it. I have also written to Governor Schwarzenegger and he has also helped me a lot too. I got a letter from him too and some e-mails. I am proud because I know that it doesnt matter what party they belong to they both care about how people are treated and how things that are wrong should be corrected. I also know that they really do care. I felt like at a time when no one really cared about how youths were treated or how one was treated by certain agencies, these guys really did care. I felt proud that they listened to me. I felt proud that they didn't dismiss me just because of my mental illness.

You know what else? I felt really proud when I graduated. I had to study almost 10 hours a day to keep up with my classes and had tutors who helped me and my therapist encouraged me. I also had a social worker who helped me and I was so proud when they were really happy for me. I know they really care about me and I know I can trust them. I feel proud at work because when I have a idea, everyone listens to me and they let me be creative. I can be me and they don't mind that I am ill. I learn a lot from them and they accept me just the way I am and that makes me proud of me.

By Anonymous

When my daughter trusted me enough to ask me to take

care of her children for a week while they were out of the country. When I went to England, Scotland and Ireland for three weeks with two guys from NAMI. Everytime I speak and someone says thank you-"you've helped me understand or you've given me hope or you've changed my opinion."
By Anonymous

What are the best books you have read on the subject? How have they helped you?

"Darkness Visible: A Memoir of Madness" by William Styron - I started reading a magazine excerpt of this when I was in the middle of my severe depression and not yet getting treatment. It was too scary and I put it down. After I started getting better, I read it all, and found it to be the best description of what I went through. I recommended to family and friends if they wanted to understand my illness. I'm not sure any of them read it.

"Night Falls Fast: understanding suicide" by Kay Redfield Jamison - I did attempt suicide during my second bout of severe depression, and after I came out of the depression, I found this to be most helpful about what I had been through. I like her honesty and candor and the fact that she still practices her profession.

"I Am Not Sick; I Don't Need Help: a Practical Guide for Families and Therapists - This book speaks to what my process actually was, and so I think it is one of the most helpful books for families and therapists; and for me to understand my original denial.

I've read many other books, and the most helpful are always people's personal stories.
By NAMISD.1.4i

What's the most encouraging illustration of support for people with mental illness that you know about?

I read about "Geel, Belgium: A Model of Community Recovery." Geel had an institution for the mentally ill and has incorporated the mentally ill into their community. People accept them, interact with them, and support them as they can.

I also really admire companies where people can be open with their bosses about their mental illness and the company keeps them on and works with and around their illness. I know of at least two such companies in San Diego, CA.
By NAMISD.1.4i

As the younger sister of someone enduring Schizophrenia, I feel as if my life is inextricably bound to another reality. Since the ten years ago brother was diagnosed, I have had the time to contemplate this new meaning of "brother," in the sense of his happiness, my happiness, and our family future roles. Through this time, I have found the "most encouraging illustration of support for the mentally ill" has been my own shift in perspective of the mentally ill.

When my brother was first diagnosed, I found that the existing societal perspective on mental illness was negative, with a dose of cloudiness. Worse yet, the Asian culture did not seem to recognize the fact at all. While my family felt ashamed and confused, an equally depressing feeling of loneliness washed over our journey to seek help. One of the hardest issues for my family was the question of why: why my brother was "different" and not "normal."

I know that my parents still carry guilt about my brother's current status. Tears will fill their eyes as they account for all the lost life experiences my brother will miss. No girlfriend. No job. No college education. No

184

independence. But more recently, I have been able to confidently tell them not to be worried or sad.

If the concept of mental illness can be viewed more broadly, I believe happiness and contentment can be found. Although the definition of mental illness almost automatically implies some sort of abnormality, it is not an immutable definition. My approach is that mental illness merely gives my brother and others the ability to experience life through another viewing lens.

When I observe my brother now, I see happiness. His happiness is derived from purchasing candy at the local store, strolling around an outdoor mall, and listening to music videos on YouTube. I see disappointment when he is refused an extra cigarette. I see excitement when he is told of an upcoming dinner event. In sum, my brother experiences life. This is his new role in life, one in which my family and society must accept.

Though he will experience life "differently" from my family, his peers, or me, I always maintain that my own ideals or societal ideals for what "life experience" holds, should not and does not translate to my brother. It is this perspective of mental illness that relieves me from worries and sadness.

I hope this approach lessens the emotional burdens of managing a loved one with mental illness. I believe that emotional confidence is important for the future advocacy and aid for the mentally ill. A portion of society with mental illness will always exist, but with inner strength and positive perspective, the journey through this new life with your loved one can be more clear and secure.
By derby1209

Is there anything else that has happened to you or that you've experienced in this area that you would like to share?

I have learned the true meaning of respect. It isn't "putting up with" or seeking to accomodate or pandering to or any of the other superficial ways that we show respect for another person. You respect someone when you can see that person as an individual with all of his strengths and weaknesses. Period. It means not judging and not comparing that person to another. It requires listening and empathy.
By 1curtis1

Things you learned

What advice would you give to a family encountering mental illness for the first time?

Get help from a medical professional right away. Then go to NAMI's Family-to-Family class. Inform yourself about the illness. Join a NAMI support group for families. As a consumer, the thing that helps me the most being around people in NAMI is that we can all talk openly and frankly about our mental illness stories. It makes such a huge difference, especially in a society that is still leery of mental illness.
By NAMISD.1.4i

Recovery is a journey, not a destination. Have patience and don't give up hope and call on your NAMI friends for support. Learn to enjoy this new person, not regret the loss of the old and above all keep a sence of humor.
By NAMISD.1.4c

Join a Family Support Group.
I would encourage a family encountering mental illness to find a good family support group right away. In my opinion, the downfall of anyone affected by mental illness, which extends to the family, is alienation. In this respect, the experience of those affected by mental illness is uniquely different from AIDS, cancer, heart disease, or other major illnesses that garner a great deal more social sympathy, understanding, and acceptance. Because this is the case, I think it is imperative for families to seek support from each other and become as educated as possible as soon as possible. In addition, a good support group will help family members learn to take care of their own needs, to set boundaries, and to relax in the company of peers.

See a Therapist:
Another necessity for families is to seek individual therapy for themselves. Mental illness truly is a "family illness." Everyone touched by it will be affected. In other words, mental illness has a tendency to bleed through the family dynamic more than other "more talked-about" illnesses and has the potential to wreak havoc. To help with this issue, a trained therapist can allow family members to vent, learn tools to cope, assist in decision making, cushion overwhelming feelings, and act as another pillar of support. A therapist can be a huge ally in conjunction with the peer support group.

Grieve:
It is important for family members to allow themselves to grieve. One of the most difficult aspects for family members is the realization that things didn't turn out the way they thought they would; things that were once normal expectations are now impossible. Mental illness can become synonymous with the loss of lifestyle, hopes and dreams, or even a loss of the identity of the loved one, the one they "knew and loved." Grieving will be long, often sporadic, but is part of the process of coping. I would advise people to expect to grieve and to grieve often.

Change Expectations:
On the other side of this coin, it is important to redefine what is considered success for the individual with the mental illness. Perhaps a new hope is simply that the individual with the diagnosis is able to demonstrate love. Perhaps the hope is that the individual has self esteem. Perhaps the goal is that the individual can find a bit of joy in life. Perhaps the hope would be just be that the individual doesn't have a bad day every so often. Whatever the case may be, the onset of a mental illness requires all family members to alter what may be well-ingrained expectations, and this promises to be another area that requires rigorous effort from family members.

Take Care of Yourself:
Next, I would evoke the age old analogy of the plane about to crash with the little oxygen bags dropping from the panel above. We have all see the cartoon drawing with the mom putting on her own mask before she assists the child. This is a corollary for the role of the family in mental illness. The only control over the situation one may have is to attend to his own security first, but in doing so, one gives the loved one better odds for a quality of life. Although this analogy is overly dramatic, I think there is truth in it. The recovery literature speaks to this point of "helping yourself first," and I would wholeheartedly agree. The more a family member takes care of himself, the more he can take care of someone else.

Recovery is Possible:
Now, the part of the above analogy that is false is that the family member and the individual with a mental illness are not in a crashing plane. The worst thing in the world has not occurred. A loved one has a mental illness, and what that means is that a loved one has a mental illness.

Mental illnesses are biological brain disorders, and the symptoms can be addressed with medication, therapy, peer support, and lifestyle choices. The struggle is undeniable, but there is much to be learned and much to

be gained from dealing with this aspect of life. The most important thing to remember is that recovery is possible!
By NAMISD.1.6h

The life lesson we have learned is, for any situation that results in a life-long condition that in any way limits a person's ability to fully function, it is crucial to face into that reality. It is then essential to be fully educated about the condition and to gather support in order to effectively reconstruct a life that is fulfilling to the utmost under the circumstances. We learned with friends who suffered the consequences of debilitating accidents, that the same elements are required.

We have also learned that methods of communication that are critical to success in dealing with someone with a mental illness are just as applicable in all relationships. Although we would not recommend it to anyone, we have definitely grown as people from living with this experience.
By Anonymous

What is the best advice someone has given you?

To not speak all the time. To listen well, and to speak only when I have something to say. To know that I am loved, and can keep telling myself that. To not bore my family and friends with all the details of my illness, but to do talk to others who understand. To be open and honest about who I am. To stand up for myself and set boundaries. That it's okay to fight or be angry and then let it go. To express my joys and sorrows appropriately. To not blame others or myself. It is not okay for someone to abuse me emotionally, and I can stand up for myself. God has forgiven me, can I forgive myself?
By NAMISD.1.4i

I was taught from an early age that consideration of others is one of the most important life traits. It is right up there with honesty and honor. As I've grown older and the people I know and meet have become more numerous and more diverse, I've learned that being considerate means restating the Golden Rule. It is not doing unto others as you would have them do unto you as we have learned since we were knee-high. Being considerate, and thus showing respect, means doing unto others as THEY would have done unto them. Not everyone's needs have the same priority as mine. Not everyone's culture and beliefs are just like mine. Not everyone is just like me. Go figure.

By 1curtis1

What do you know today you wish you had known on the day you were diagnosed?

I wish I had known that the sooner I accepted my illness the sooner I would get better.

I wish I had known the meaning of the word "chronic." My doctor told me that having a mental illness was like "being a person in their 50's with a heart condition." I was 19 years old at the time and had no way of comprehending what that meant. I wish I had.

I wish I had known someone who was living well with a mental illness. It took me nearly a decade to find such a person, someone in my support group who had bipolar disorder who had not had a major episode in eight years. This was unbelievable! I befriended this person, and he gave me hope. I just wish I had known to join a support group sooner.

I wish I had known that I would turn out just fine. I have had to change my expectations of happiness and march to the beat of a different drummer. I wish I had known that this would be the best way of living for me whether I was a person with a diagnosis or not.

I wish I had known at the time that I would develop courage. Any person who decides to do battle with a mental illness needs courage to make it through. I wish I had known that courage, as well as many other virtues, would be the byproduct of doing battle with mental illness. I wish I knew that I would become a person to be proud of.
By NAMISD.1.6h

What have you learned about people and our society as a result of this condition?

I have learned through my own personal experience, and years of work in advocacy with NAMI that most people who haven't been touched by a mental illness are woefully ignorant about it. The discussion is much better now than it has ever been, but there is still a lot of stigma, ignorance, and misinformation. We did pass the mental health parity bill, which was a huge step, but people still tend to think that a mental illness is not a physical illness and that somehow we who are mentally ill are to blame for our condition. Or at least our families are. As a society, we still do not have a commitment to health care for all, much less mental health care for all. Our treatment of mental illness is so sporadic and scattered. We do not seem to have a way to promulgate what really works to other areas. We do not have an overall system that ties together. The burden is on the patient and the family to find their way through the maze at a time when they are most vulnerable. But I do have a lot of hope, because the more people truly understand, the more they are compassionate.
By NAMISD.1.4i

As it relates to mental illness do you continue to learn? If so, in what ways?

I have learned that mental illness, especially depression is related to other major medical conditions. One important one is Heart Disease. Of the medical professionals I have "surveyed" each believed that Depression was a significant a risk factor for Heart Disease as high blood pressure or high cholesterol. Yikes!
By Anonymous

Management and Recovery

Things that happened

What resources have you used to deal with mental illness and which do you value most?

I always had my parents to guide me. My dad passed away and that was hard, but I remebered all the advice he gave me and the things he taught me and that helped me a lot. My psychiatrist and my therapist are my most helpful "friends" they listened to me, they treat me like a real person, they go to bat for me and mostly when I wanted to die, my psychiatrist yelled, not really loud, at me one day and made me promise not to try to kill myself again, so I promised and have never done that again. I know he cares, I've been seeing him 30 years or so, and he and my therapist taught me a lot and always had faith in me, just like my dad. They never get mad at me and they are always there for me, and that makes my life and my sadness easier to deal with. I respect them and their opinion matters to me a lot. They have never given me bad advice. They are they for the good times and the bad times. When I need them, they are always there, they call me right back and they help me feel special when I am sad or sick. They help me with everything. They are also proud of me and never push me to do anything until I am ready. They care about me a lot, just like my dad did. My mom taught me how to stick up for myself. She and I have had a harder relationship. I used to think she didn't love me, but now I know she does. I really had to work hard to make things get better between my mom and me. She doesn't show affection or tell you how great you are, but she is more critical, but now I understand all that and so I feel better. I also know that due to her background, this is

193

how she was raised and loves me despite her upbringing. It took me a long time to understand her, years and years, but I wouldn't trade her for anything in the world.
By NAMISD.1.5a

Can you describe the first time you felt like you had turned the corner towards getting your life under control?

The first time was when my husband was away for a sustained period of time, and I realized that life could be calm, I could be productive, and my children could express themselves freely without the constraints of the illness.
By Anonymous

I was visiting my dad in another state. I asked him, "How does it feel to know your daughter is crazy?" He said, "How does it feel to know your dad is dying from cancer?" Wait, before you cry, let me explain to you something. "Your mother and I knew you had problems before we adopted you." Then he told me this... He said, "We didn't ask for our diseases, you and I. But we must learn to live with them. No one asks for a disease. Unlike others, we can't run and hide. We can't claim ignorance and we can't ignore the hardships these diseases put on us. We must learn to control the disease so the disease doesn't control us. We must let others get to know us for ourselves, and then let them learn about our disease so in this way we can teach others the truth about the illnesses we didn't deserve or ask for, but we have to live with. In this way, we can become teachers and help others understand what the truths are." My dad was a very wise man. He worked with people with lot of trouble. He and my mom taught me to not judge others. They said, prejudice was wrong. They said by not giving anyone a chance you could lose a friend you never got to meet. My dad had his own stories, but he never made me feel like I was less. Sadly, it was

shortly after my visit he passed away. It was then I began getting control of my life. My son got in trouble with the law, things weren't going right for him and all my dad's wisdom came back to me. I fought for my son and I learned a lot. I returned to school to rebuild my life. I took my dad's advice, if you're going to do something do your best or don't do it. I graduated with honors. It was only an AA degree, but I still live by all the things my mom and dad taught me. My step-mom taught me some things too. I once asked my dad why somethings were unfair, and he said if everyone could pick their problems, everyone would pick the easy ones. He told me Challange and acceptance are won by all things not easy. To overcome the things we cannot control makes us stronger and wiser as time goes on. It is up to us to help eachother.
By NAMISD.1.5a

Is there anything else that has happened to you or that you've experienced in this area that you would like to share?

Not every medication works for everyone. Keep a journal of how you feel each day. If something doesn't feel right or you are having thoughts that frighten you call your doctor right away!
By Anonymous

When I feel really sad or like I have made mistakes, it hurts inside. If I lose a friend it hurts a lot. But, when I cry at home, my son always says, "Mom I love you." "I will always be here for you, even though I tease you and don't show it." He can make me feel better. He can make me laugh. He tells me about his teasing me. He says "Mom, I know your a good person." He stands up for me when I am hurt. My doctor and my therapist are always there for me too. They remind me of all the good things I do. I think it is easy to give up sometimes. But, I try to remember who to call and they are there for me. When it is night time, I watch my tv and sometimes just cry and sometimes I let my illness make me talk to myself to sort things out. I know I have to be here for the people I volunteer for and for my son. I know that I want to make sure I can make everyone proud of me.

I also have a cat. She is really good and I know she wouldn't be loved by anyone else so I know I have to get through my illness. Sometimes I dream about my dad, and I always have really great dreams. I can interact with my dreams and I love them. I know I can dream away my bad feelings. I know my son needs me. I know no one else will love him like me and my mom. I have to be good so he can have a good future. I like what my dad told me once, that if you try to change others, you don't know who they are anymore. I guess I think it is most important to know that you will fit in and be ok, it may not always seem like it but sometimes people like me don't get to be really good untill we get older.

I was never great in school, but my therapist and my psychiatrist taught me how to find my good points, strengths, and how to use those things to feel good about myself. I wasn't a real good daughter to my dad, but I try to be a great daughter for my mom. I know everyone has problems, but when it seems like my problems are the only ones, I try to think about all the good things I know. I try to feel like I can talk to my cat and she doesn't care if I am ugly or fat or icky and sick. I think it is important to know that you can make a difference for someone else even by just saying hello. If we don't give of ourselves, then we might have missed a chance to help someone else. We are special and even though we don't always feel like we are, we can reach out and be there for someone else. Maybe that's why we go through so much so we can help others.

By Anonymous

Things you learned

In your opinion, is recovery possible? Why do you believe that?

For Bipolar Disorder I feel it is not possible to recover. Even on the best medications, biweekly visits to my psychiatrist, weekly visits with a therapist, regular trips to my doctor and a great support network I still have break through episodes that defy all attempts to control them. But I feel you can manage it and expect that there will be times when things won't go so well. Even after trying lots of medications I know that the best regimen can fall apart. But it's absolutely necessary to work closely with a doctor or psychiatrist to monitor, track and update your meds and to learn to be very self aware so you bring things to their attention. There is no 'getting over' something like Bipolar. It's for life and it can get worse. You have break through episodes despite the best medications and care.

The real 'recovery' is in learning to believe in your doctors and your family and any others you trust to be there for you and to help you when things do happen. Having people in your life who know about your illness and who care about you and want to help you is the most important thing because when episodes do occur they will be the only thing normal in your life.
By NAMISD.1.1d

Because there is nothing that GOD can not do!
By NAMISD.1.3d

Definitely! I believe that recovery from mental illness is like that of any illness, that it takes a lot support, people willing to listen, people to allow you to take one step forward and sometimes two steps back. That recovery can be a bit of a rollercoaster, but the ride can slow down. I believe it because they are so many people who have faced the amazing challenge that mental illness brings and who have created what they wanted/desired out of their life, which is something I think we are all striving to do. Many times it seems that those who are not on the road to recovery are still on the fast-paced rollercoaster because they have encountered uncaring and unwilling caregivers. That their hope was taken away from them somewhere along this journey. If we can give them back their hope, their independence, their respect, I believe recovery is possible.

By NAMISD.1.1f

How have you managed to bring yourself up from the bottom?

A firm belief in being responsible for my life to the best of my ability has kept me going during even the darkest of moments. I want to live a life well lived, a life with no regrets. That means staying alive even when I want to give up. To live a life of excellence with a serious, severe mental illness means to always be alert to the dangers of instability, its causes and its reasons. Virtue in action with a serious mental illness means a constant monitoring of stress, sleep, emotions, mental and physical well being, doctor appointments, psychology appointments, and all the many aspects of maintaining wellness.

By Anonymous

How have you gained more control over your condition?

Sobriety, medication, GOD, and good desicions.

By NAMISD.1.3d

What are the most important element(s) to recovery?

If there was a pill to take to make it all feel better, everyone would be taking it. I believe and always have that medications can be a lifesaver. But medications are only part of the recovery, therapy and counseling are how we recover and/or learn to live with what we have. To understand what we will face we need to gain understanding of ourselves and our illness. That doesn't come in a pill form. It also takes work. But it is worth it.
By Anonymous

What roles do family, friends, work, faith and medicine have in recovery?

Faith and family play a huge role in recovery. The love and support of my family is a every day joy. A strong connection with GOD is the most imortant and vital tool.
By NAMISD.1.3d

I think recovery is an on-going thing. My friends well they come and go but the people I work with where I volunteer are good people and they are always nice to me. They make me feel good. I love them and I know they like what I do. I made some friends there and they make me feel important and special. I have made some really good friends too, some that are there for me no matter how kooky I am. My family is important because I don't want to let them down. My brother tries to understand mental illness but he doesn't really understand it. I guess I made him so upset in earlier years that he is just disgusted. I keep trying to get him to understand though. I see him as a project in work. He loves me I think, but he needs a little bit of fine tuning.

I studied world religion and I believe in many different things so I hold onto my beliefs. I really treasure the cultures of people and why they believe what they believe. I find it interesting and I have met some very nice people. I love to listen to people teach me about things I don't understand because it helps me find myself a little bit more.

I take my medicine faithfully. I sometimes hate it because I think yeah this little pill is going to make me feel better? RIGHT...but then I take it and a while later I wonder why I was so upset. I remember the first time I took psychiatric medicine, it was sort of frightening. I thought, what if it makes me different, what if I don't know who I am anymore. I thought what if I can't remember the things I want to remember? But I trusted my psychiatrist and finally tried the medicine. It didn't make me different, but it did help me have better days after a while. I used to take a lot of different ones, but now I don't. It takes a while to find the right one to take, but, it does help and if you keep on it and talk to your Doctor, you will find the right stuff, it tooks me years but now I am glad I stuck it out, I'm not saying it was easy or that even now I got the perfect medication, but I can deal with things better and I do have better days just like my psychiatrist said I would.

I know how important medicine is but you still need to see a therapist to make it work out ok. I am honest with my therapist and even when I am wrong she doesn't judge me, she helps me see how I can improve and helps me see the truth.

My life hasn't been easy by any means, it seems like I always get the unusual problems, the worst situations, and the hardest decisions to make, but once a boss told me that he gave me the hardest guys to deal with because he had faith in me that I could do a great job with them. I remember that because sometimes what I learn helps others and I like to help other people.

At one time I wanted to die, but like my psychiatrist said, now I am really glad I didn't die. It took me a long time to find a place I could be happy and now I wouldn't trade any of my life for anything! Even when I am sad, I know that the universe, or God, or whatever you believe in has a plan for you and it is up to you to stick it out and find the answers.

I think life is like a present, I get to see what I got at the end of the day and if I don't like it, then in the morning I get a new present to open up as the day goes on. You can sleep away a bad day, and sometimes you can find a great present the next day so just do the best you can and that is good enough. You can win if you play, but you can't win if you don't play. So, even though it may take a long time, you will find many good gifts in your life. Then you can share them and be proud of yourself.
By Anonymous

What is the most important skill or attitude you have learned in dealing with mental illness?

The most important skill was patience, the most important attitude was that there is no normal, and that each of us can discover multiple strengths and experiment with new ways of being in the world in order to find what most enhances our own vitality and our own 'normal'.
By Anonymous

For me, the most important attitudes have been understanding the illness and then accepting it. It may not seem that understanding something can be an attitude, but for me it was. It was hard to understand something when I couldn't even fathom it's existence, let alone believe it may be a part of my own life. I had to learn that it was "ok" to have a mental disability. I spent my teenage years and the early part of my twenties not realizing I had mild depression. In fact, during those years, the depression may have been more severe. I started to understand that I may have it during my thirties but wasn't very knowledgable about how the disease can manifest itself in individuals. I thought that if I really had depression, then I'd be suicidal or catatonic all the time. I needed to the accept the subtlies of the illness. I began to learn how it can have a variety of symptoms from person to person. My own symptoms often changed as well. In my forties, I learned to accept it, nurture myself during the bad times and not take criticism so personally when it came from my family. My immediate family accepted me for the most part. I do not discuss it with my extended family to this day.

By NAMISD.1.2e

A belief in, and practice of compassion, love, and thoughtfulness perpetuates more of the same. As each of us becomes saturated in this realization and puts into daily practice the art of love and compassion, the world is a brighter, better place for all of us.

By Anonymous

What else is important to recovery? Are there any other things that you have learned about this topic that you would like to share with us? What are we not asking you, that we should be asking you, if we knew to ask it?

I firmly believe we were created to be interdependent to assist, support and encourage one another. To find our purpose in this world we need to seek out where we can be of service, and deal with our challenges in order to make a difference in the world. By believing in one another, each and every one of us becomes the difference that one person can make in the life of another. Even though our talents and gifts are not all the same, each of us is uniquely gifted and each of us has meaning and purpose. Sometimes we lose sight of that. My biggest take away from my experience is that we are all interconnected, that each of us is unique and we need to value that uniqueness in others. We are dependent upon one another for our purpose, for our meaning, for our reason for living. We exist to help and love one another. It's in the sharing of our lives where we really help each other. Sharing your story is a gift that you give others that brings meaning to all of our lives. Do not suffer alone or in silence. Reach out. Call a doctor. Call a friend. Call a loved one. Call a hot line.

By Anonymous

NAMI & Other Support Organizations

Things that happened

How did you first hear about NAMI (or support organizations like NAMI)?

It all started with my mom, who was the first and only in my family to complete the Family to Family class. She shared with me that there was an organization called NAMI that helped people with a diagnosed mental illness. Then she gently pointed me to the Peer to Peer class that NAMI offers for free. Her commercial did not make a significant impression until I saw a flier for the class on the desk where I volunteered months later. I knew then it was time for me to join the class and from there on I got more and more into NAMI San Diego.
By NAMISD.1.4h

When I went back to school, my one of my tutors told me about NAMI. My therapist had told me about it before, but I wasn't too interested. Anyway, my tutor told me about a class there called Peer to Peer. I finally went and it was good. For the first time, I really felt like my problems werent just my own, that other people had the same problems as me. That I was ok too. The mentors I had in my class were really nice. I really like my Doctor and my therapist, but also the support groups helped me a lot. I could meet other people with problems and we could all brainstorm and find answers to our problems. It takes a while to feel comfortable sometimes, but a group can really help you. Keep all your appt's and be yourself.

You will learn that others will accept you if you accept yourself.

By Anonymous

One of the members of my Bi-Polar support group told me about NAMI. She was an IOOV speaker and thought I should take the speaker training.

By NAMISD.1.4c

Did you know about mental health support organizations before the diagnosis of mental illness? If you learned about them after a diagnosis, how long after?

I did not know about any mental health support organizations before my diagnosis. I learned about them a couple years later from my mother.

By NAMISD.1.3d

Is there anything else that has happened to you or that you've experienced in this area that you would like to share?

I took the IOOV training in Jan. 2000 and have been presenting ever since. I find telling my story has given me understanding, forgiveness, and compassion for myself and others with mental illness as well as there families.

I have been a help line operator and was on staff as Volunteer Coordinator for two years. I have been the NAMI San Diego IOOV Coordinator for four years, State Trainer for three and National Trainer for one year.

I was fortunate to be able to speak before The Senate Hearing on Older Adult Depression, Suicide and Violence. Medicare part D was one outcome of the committee

I love helping make a difference in people's lives and the NAMI family is a tremendous support system for me and others.. I am proud to be associated with them.
By Anonymous

Things you learned

What role has NAMI (or other support organizations) played in your life?

NAMI and other oganizations such as RICA have played a major role in my life of recovery. They have support groups, trainings, classes, and knowledge about recovery.
By NAMISD.1.3d

I feel like NAMI saved my life. Not only did I get my life back, I got a better me...one I understand and like. I feel fortunate to be able to work for NAMI San Diego.

I have attended support groups and found that, unlike other groups I had attended, I was able to cut to bottom line and get to action I need to make change.

Working on the Information and Referral Line helped me really learn to listen and helped me learn about what was and was not available in our community. That experience spurred me to become an advocate for better health care services in our community. As a result I have worked on legislation and was very active on the Prop 63 commitee - to get it passed and to develop programs to use the money once we got it.

As Volunteer Coordinator I was able to develpoe mentoring skills and found patience, compassion and understanding for myself and others with mental illness.

As a presenter and trainer for "In Our Own Voice" I continue to learn about my illness. I am reminded by other presenters about coping skills, and my audience about the difference I am making in people's lives.
By NAMISD.1.4c

What role has NAMI or a similar organization played in your or your loved ones recovery?

After many frustrating encounters with the field of psychiatric medicine we were extremely disappointed and overwhelmed by the lack of constructive help. What turned out to be the most important positive step we took was to get connected with NAMI, which we accomplished by attending a national convention in Chicago. We then realized there were thousands of people throughout the nation dissatisfied with the services they were receiving (or not) and banding together to confront the inadequate system. For the first time we felt some hope. This was seven years after the onset of our son's paranoid Schizophrenia, three years during which he was homeless.

We became immersed in NAMI activities, including monthly meetings with highly motivated NAMI members, attending additional national conventions and becoming involved in the Mental Health service system as board members of service providers. In addition we attended a community college course, SMI 101. All these activities led us to acceptance of our son's illness and connected us to a network that opened up possibilities that we had no knowledge of, and to advocacy for those suffering from these debilitating disorders. Through the network we were able to connect our son to a private case worker who tracked him for several years until we could connect him with services which led to him accepting treatment. Our son finally accepted taking medication enabling him to become stable enough to acquire a part time job, which he has now held for over 14 years, while living on his own, and growing more stable during that time.

By Anonymous

What's the most important thing that you've learned from organizations like NAMI or have gotten from them?

I have learned from NAMI that I am not alone in my pain anymore. When I first began the Peer to Peer class, I found myself around people that understood what I was going through because they went through almost the same thing. NAMI gave me strength to share my experience in other communities because I know I have my own community of consumers behind me. I would not have known about that force if not for NAMI San Diego. I now facilitate their weekly support group called Connection and I see the same thing happening for others.

By NAMISD.1.4h

The Most Important Lessons We've Learned

During the course of the initial project documenting experiences and lessons learned from mental illness one idea was suggested so often that we decided to make it part of all future projects. The idea was this – conclude the book with a chapter on personal growth and gratitude. The logic behind this idea was as follows. After we had taken the time to think about what we had lived through and reflect on what we had learned from our encounters with mental illness, we had come to a near universal conclusion. We realized that the challenges we faced had, whether directly or indirectly, caused us to grow as human beings in ways that we would not have grown otherwise. Without these provocations, these difficulties in our lives, we would not have become the people we became, and missing that opportunity for personal, psychological, social, emotional and spiritual growth would have been a loss. In short, we didn't enjoy the trip, but we were very grateful for the destination where we had arrived. With that gratitude in mind we wanted to use the last chapter in the book to share our realizations and lessons learned, no matter what the subject, to encourage and give hope to those who will travel this road in the future.

So, with that explanation, we hope you enjoy this final chapter on the most important lessons we've learned.

209

Me in a Relationship

What was the first serious relationship you ever had? Who was it with, how did you meet and get together, what was the attraction, how long did it last, and how did it end?

Thomas still looms large in my mind's eye. No one ever moved me the way he did. No one ever held my attention like he did. He was my first true love. I worshiped the ground he walked on.

Thomas and I first met in the hallway in front of our Latin class at UCSD. The class was incredibly difficult, the students competitive, and the class size intimate. There was always a group of us sitting out in front of the classroom, exchanging translations, commiserating, and sometimes bitching, at least an hour before the class started. I liked to sit in the hallway and write in my journal. (I kept a journal religiously at the time to cope with my father's suicide three months prior.) Thomas liked to pace in the hallway and give all those seated "lectures" on literature, philosophy, and politics. I thought he was arrogant, imperious, and downright insufferable.

Occasionally, Thomas and I would exchange smart remarks, and unlike other members of the class, I didn't have trouble tangling with him or sassing him back. However, the students were soon to discover just how smart Thomas really was. He was by far and away the best student in the class, as excellent as I was mediocre. Because of his Latin prowess, he gained the respect of everyone, and by the end of the quarter, Thomas was considered a minor deity among the Latin dilettantes.

The final in the class was unbearable to me for reasons that I didn't understand. I did well, but I sensed that something was wrong. I was SO...happy...spacey....gone? Less than 12 hours after the I completed my exam, I was hospitalized for a manic episode due to bipolar disorder and was put on lithium.

After my "vacation," I returned to school thrashed, depressed, and medicated. I didn't really know what bipolar disorder was, only that I had completely snapped. Returning to my Latin class seemed insurmountable; the level of memorization was so intense that I didn't know how I was going pass, much less get a good grade.

One day I was walking to dinner on the Revelle College campus on my way to the cafeteria for dinner when I ran into Thomas. He was hard to miss, tall and broad, wearing all black, black hair, striking blue eyes, carrying a heavy, well-used backpack. We both stopped. The next thing I knew, I asked him to join me for dinner, and he accepted.

Our first real conversation, as many that followed, I remember specific bits of dialog. In this conversation, he asked me "what had happened to me" over the break. "You're different," he observed. "Really different."

I gave him a thumbnail sketch of my experience, short but honest. He said, "So, you're on lithium?" I affirmed. He continued, "I've been on lithium for the past two years. I'm a manic, too." So that explained it, the lecturing, the intensity, the...affinity?

But our affinity went well beyond a mere diagnosis. As Thomas once said to me later, "to find all of the connections between us would require an archeologist." We had long talks, long walks, long coffee dates, and over that year, we became inseparable. I cut his hair. He read his poetry. We listened to music. We went to the beach at night, we studied Latin by day. With his help, even in spite of a lacerated rote memory, I was able to do well in all my classes.

In the end, though, it was my anticipated trip to England that drove us apart. Before I met Thomas, I had applied to go to England with the education abroad program. It was in the Spring that I got my letter and discovered that I had been accepted. I was ambivalent. I wanted Thomas to tell me not to go.

Instead, he told me to go. He told me that he didn't want the responsibility of holding me back from something I wanted. I really wanted to be held back; he was more important. But he was adamant, so I left for England with my joy sullied by the relationship that might have been. When I returned, he went off to Stanford for graduate school, and I had already entered another relationship with a boy from England.

Thomas and I always kept in touch. His deep voice and sinister laugh were still a constant presence in my life, even as we both moved forward.

As time went on, though, I witnessed Thomas' mental illness undermine his intellect, as well as his basic reasoning, and eventually his survival instinct. In the last year of his graduate work, Thomas lost his mind completely and took his own life. He left me a box of his poetry to publish after his death, which now resides in a storage unit. The poems are too painful to read. There was also a note.

Someday I will open the poems and read them, and I will be able to handle the tears, though their water would be enough to fill a thousand oceans.

Looking back on this situation, I realize that I let Thomas make my decision to go to England for me. He told me to go; I went. I thought his opinion about *my* destiny was more valid than my own because in my heart of hearts I wanted to stay. Because I looked up to Thomas, I gave him the authority to make a decision that would have shaped both of our lives. I wonder now...What if he had come around? What if he really didn't want me to go, but would have felt guilty discouraging me from my dream?

What if he didn't mean what he said when he said he wanted me to go? Now, I will never know.

Ultimately, I've learned that just because a person in authority--authority by your choosing or otherwise--says I should do something doesn't necessarily mean it's what I should do. I'm still learning to listen to myself, even when my voice is contrary to those I love and respect the most.

Though he intended to accomplish this another way, Thomas would be proud to know that he taught me this life lesson, to march to the beat of my own drummer.
By Anonymous

What did you learn from watching your parents' marriage? What parts of their relationship and behavior have you tried to emulate and what parts have you vowed never to repeat?

My parents have now been married 53 years. That number alone is something to be admired without even knowing the details of their marriage. I am very proud of them in many areas, especially in their marriage. I look back now and realize how much I did pick up as a child while living with them. It all seemed so "normal" at the time although now I can take a more critical look at some of those memories. My parents were completely devoted to each other and it was obvious that the kids were really a distant second to their relationship. I view that as a very healthy dynamic. I also remember that my dad made the decisions. None of us would question his choices, not even my mother. My mom was kind of a go-between for us and our dad. She took care of all the smaller issues in life and he made the bigger decisions. My mom rarely intervened once he decided to do something. But, when she did, my dad acquiesed willingly. This almost always surprised me

213

because of the narrow view I had of my dad being the "power" in the family. I realize now that there was more shared power than I knew. I know my mom still felt that she didn't know how to make decisions after being married to such a strong man. She made that statement to me over 20 years ago. I knew I didn't want to feel that way while I was married.

Here I am in my own marriage of 23 years. I would certainly say that my husband I have a more balanced marriage that way. Each of us has our strengths and each are more comfortable making decisions in those areas. Occasionally we step on each other's toes when we both feel strongly about an issue but it seems that happens less and less as time goes by. I do feel that I could make good decisions even if something happened to my husband. I don't look forward to it certainly because I like letting him take care of certain things in our life.

I do remember hearing people comment about their parent's fighting. I never heard mine do that. As I explained above, it is clear why they didn't quarrel. There is nothing to fight about when one person is making all the decisions. I don't think our two children can say they never heard us argue. I know they did but that's ok in my book. There was never any violence, we never involved the kids and we are still together today. I hope that is a good role model for them.
By NAMISD.1.2e

Belonging, Connection & Traditions

How have you overcome the feeling that you don't belong, and how have you helped others over this hurdle?

I never really felt I belonged once I started school. The kids picked on me a lot. They beat me up, called me names and said terrible things to me. I never really told anyone about it, I just knew somehow that this was not something I could explain. I had Mommy, Daddy, and my brother. However, the kids at school out-numbered my family. I believed the terrible things they said. My whole life, I looked for proof that my family couldn't possibly love me. I thought I was perfect in one respect, yet I had no self-confidence and I was afraid of failing.

As I got older, things got worse. I didn't fit in and I wasn't popular. I was blaming my family for making me go to school. I was a horrible daughter, and sister to my brother. I was a year and half older so I could beat up my brother really good. I did that a lot. I was so hurt inside and so angry that no one seemed to want to be my friend because the bullies never let up. I wanted to die. My parents made sure my teachers gave me time to learn and extra help. I had a hard time keeping up with studies. My dad hired a private tutor for me and made sure she could also be supportive to my feelings and help me feel better about myself. Yet, I still had a rage in me. I took it out on my family. No one else knew how I felt inside. I wanted to hurt my family and prove that they couldn't love me. I couldn't stop. I would feel terrible and swear that it wouldn't happen again. But I couldn't stop.

After I had my son, I really tried to be a good mommy. One night I was crying. I told my son I was a big fat nothing. That no one could ever love me and that I really had tried to be a good daughter and sister. Then he said, "Mom, you know how sometimes when we argue and you say you don't care?" I said "yes, but I don't mean it." Well, he said, "I know that. Why do you think we don't love you?" I said "because I am a rotten person, I am all screwed up." He said "Mom, that's just in your head. Everyone says things they don't mean sometimes, but you know that even though they say that, you know they still care about you." Well, I thought about that for days, and then it occured to me, MY FAMILY DID LOVE ME! They really did.

I had let the bad guys take away my self worth. My whole world changed and on my mom's birthday, I told her I did love her, that I looked for proof that she didn't love me or care. I explained it all and said I was sorry and that now I finally understood how much she loved me and I loved her. She smiled at me. I spent half a century trying to prove that I didn't belong. And I lost a lot to the bullies. Now I can look back and see all the love my mom gave me, how she never gave up on me, and how my therapist and psychiatrist a well as my brother and my son let me find my way back. I am truly lucky that now, I can be me, the real me that was lost for a long time. The me I had to find.

I also have to say, my friends and everyone I worked with taught me so much. I am sure they don't know how much they gave me. I love my work, the people I work with, even though it is a volunteer job, I am so happy and I can never express how much I care about them all. I draw on my experiences to help others. I know what it is like to want to go away, but stay, because YOU ARE SPECIAL.

You get today to make mistakes and learn. Yes it is hard and sometimes painful. It is a struggle that will never end, but you are needed by someone who needs your help. You see, all the pain you have will give you strength, and give you gifts that no one else can share the way you can. You have to get throught today, it's just one day ok? You have to because you need to be here to help someone special in the future. You were aked for by special request and only you can reach out in your own special way. The future awaits you, and trust me, you are needed, wanted, and appreciated. You are special and you will know that for yourself one day in the future.

What you give will be given to the next person to help them, what a gift you have to offer. What hard lessons we learn so that the people we care about that we haven't

216

met yet will cherish all we give. You will make a difference in another person's life. Today is just one day, good, bad, or ugly....but tomorrow is a new day. You can start over, and that is what counts. I didn't have much faith in myself, but I have found it. Give yourself a chance to get better with age. The best things in life are coming your way. You are the future and you will be rewarded in time. You are important and here by special request!

By Anonymous

When do you feel most hopeless or alone, and what have you done to get through those times?

I think I get most hopeless when things don't go my way. I hate to admit it, but even as a grown man I can turn into a spoiled brat sometimes. I try to keep that part of my personality hidden, but I'm not sure how good of job I do of that all the time. When I start sinking into this abyss of my personal pity party I try to think of all the things in life that I do have, of how fortunate I have been, and of all the people I have known who have blessed me immeasurably and made my life worth living. This isn't an exercise in positive self-talk. It's an acknowledgement of a fact that I have come to know and understand over the course of my life.

Statistically, in my early 50's I'm now past the halfway mark. The greatest joy and gift of my life is something I have really only come to appreciate in the last five or so years and it's the people who I have known, worked with and lived with. I have been lucky enough to meet some of the most decent and admirable people imaginable from all across the world. These people have inspired me, loved me, encouraged me, and kept me going just by being who they are. As time goes on I have come to realize that it's not that I've somehow located all the good ones. To the contrary the point is the overwhelming majority of people out there are GOOD. There are a lot of smucks to be sure, but the world is full of wonderful, decent, caring people and the more I know them and the more of them I meet, the more I feel the need to elevate my behavior and expand my capacity for compassion to meet the bar that they have set. That can be a high bar to live up to, but when you get focused on looking up it's a lot harder to look down.

By Anonymous

What is the most important thing you have learned about connecting with people and what impact has this had on you?

I have learned that everyone we meet will contribute something to our lives. Both good and not so good. The good we enjoy and the not so good is to somehow teach us something we will need in the future. There is a light at the end of the tunnel but I couldn't find the switch. I must admit that I am not sure how I have been able to meet the wonderful people I know. I had such a naive way of looking at life. I also had a negative outlook. I once heard a speaker say that all the pain we go through is unbearable at times because it is like giving birth to a baby. We give birth to ourselves through pain so that we can experience the good things and appreciate them. Learning about ourselves is a hard, full time job. It is never ending and we need other people to help us.

I have a slice of heaven in my volunteer work. After many years of not having many friends, I now have the greatest friends one could possible hope for. I am so grateful for them. These people whom I admire and look up to, accept me even with my illness and funny ways. They gave me a chance, they have taught me a lot and they don't even know how much they have given to me! They think I am helping them, but they make my world rock, big time.

I can look back now in my life and say, you know what??? For this, it was all worth it. It is a dream come true. Ok, I had to get old and grow up, go through extreme horse pucky and listen to my therapist and doctor. I had to deal with bull dinky and stink pots for a long time. I always tried to do the right thing. That can be painful at times but I do sleep well when I sleep. Oh sure, I still have my bad hair, bad attitude and why can't the world just pop and go away days. But, I also have my "holy-smookerinie" days now too. I am so glad I am here now, I made it.

I asked my dad once why I always seemed to have the worst luck and problems and he said, don't you know? If we could pick our problems, everybody would pick only the easy ones. My parents taught me a lot of morals and values. How to treat others and how real unconditional love works.

You wouldn't believe this, but somehow, in the past, I always got the short end of the stick, well, I got a whole stick now! I can accept me now and I am glad I am here today. It took me a really long time and a lot of pain to understand my life, but I couldn't have done it without the guidance and encouragement of all the people I have met and who have taught me so much. They have been here for me and have given me so much that I will be forever in their debt. I feel honored to have them in my life and more so to have the pleasure of their support. I couldn't have asked for anything better. I truly have very caring friends and family in my life. I have truly found the most wonderful people on earth. I value each and everyone of them. They are always in my thoughts, and ofcourse they have a special place in my heart.
By Anonymous

Contrary to popular belief, I've learned that connecting with people can often be based on what you don't have in common. There is much to be gained from befriending people who have different politics, religion, ethnicity, sexual orientation, or just plain difference of opinion. After all, some of my best friends are Republicans! ;) I think it is challenging and fascinating to have people in my life who see the world a different way and aren't shy about calling me to task to defend my position or to scrutinize my own beliefs, even when on a certain topic I may wholeheartedly disagree with them.

A perfect example of this in my life is my relationship with my significant other. He is adamant about his beliefs, so adamant that he has a framed picture of Ronald Reagan in his office. Now, I am a child of the Reagan era and grew up in a Republican household, but let's just say I lean a little to the left. My SO is extremely informed, does heavy reading, and is not just a political drone. He definitely has his own opinions, some of which I feel are just flat wrong, but nonetheless, it works.
By NAMISD.1.6h

Conflicts & Confrontation

How and when did you learn to separate your emotions from your objectives? What have you done to manage, control or remove your emotions from a conflict so as not to make the situation worse? How do you 'count to 10'? Has this benefited your relationships?

I often say I have scar tissue on my tongue. I've found that one of the most important ways of learning to separate emotions from objectives is simply not saying everything I'm thinking/feeling at the moment I'm thinking/feeling it. This gives me the ability to step back and evaluate my own reactions, as well as listen fully to another person's point of view. Then, this "hold your tongue" idea goes hand in hand with "it's not about you."

For me, this was a hard lesson to learn, particularly when I felt my "self expression" and "sense of humor" was at stake. I have a dry, sarcastic sense of humor, and I was fond of showing off my cleverness. But my attitude changed dramatically during one encounter. I was hoping to move up the ladder of leadership in an organization when the current leader expressed concerns that I often "over-communicated" and tended to have a myopic perspective which started and ended with myself. This was hard to hear. I badly wanted more responsibility. Although I didn't agree entirely with this assessment and thought, to some extent, that the individual telling me this just didn't have a sense of humor, the point was taken. I stopped interjecting my opinions/humor into the group to a great extent.

The amazing benefit was that I found myself listening more and therefore having a more objective and balanced view of the members of the organization. I found that by listening more, I did have something more valuable to say when I did speak up, and as a result, I started to depersonalize others' comments and events. This "objectivity" flowed over into other aspects of my life and was a boon for personal relationships as well as my relationship with myself.

I've also learned that living with a more objective frame of mind is much less stressful than living the "it's all about me" life. The inner turbulence of emotions that are constantly triggered by the self and others is draining. I've found that by keeping my own opinions in check, that it has had the amazing result of allowing myself to see things more clearly and live a more peaceful life.
By NAMISD.1.6h

What have you learned from conflicts and from working through them that you probably could not have learned another way?

It takes two people to fight. You don't ever have to fight back. You can always choose not to "play." I used to get so incensed when my first wife would make these inflammatory statements to me about something that I felt was totally unfair or unjust. Whenever this happened I felt like I had to respond and set her straight. I had to defend myself. Of course that always led to knock down drag out fights that left me miserable, enraged and frustrated.

One day in counseling the psychologist looked at me after I had described this pattern of behavior and he said 'you see that door over there?' I said yes. He said 'pull it closed without latching it, and go stand outside the door'. I did what he told me to and felt pretty silly standing out in the hall. Then he said "now lean on the door with all your weight." And I said, "but I'll fall in and land flat on my face." To which he replied – "exactly." "If you don't push against her, she'll fall flat on her face, at which point she'll get up and say or do something more inflammatory to get you to push back against her, and when she does you keep doing what you're doing. No matter how hard she pushes or what she says just don't give her anything to push back against, and by doing that you'll forever determine whether she is just trying to get your goat, or she really wants to resolve an issue. If she's just trying to drive you nuts, she won't quit. If she wants to make things better, she'll realize that you're working to avoid a fight and are acting in good faith, and things should be able to improve."

I tried it. It worked perfectly. She was just trying to infuriate me, and would go to insane lengths to drive me to violent outbursts. You see if she could make me enraged then I would become the bad guy and she would be justified in leaving the marriage, having her affairs, etc. I refused to give her anymore justification, and even though the marriage ended I must confess that I took a certain pleasure in watching her drive herself crazy trying to get me to play her game.
By Anonymous

222

Authority Figures

When you were a child growing up, who in your life represented the epitome of authority? Who was in command of your environment, and what impact did they have on you?

THE MOM
My mother was the epitome of authority in my life growing up. In fact, the answer to that often-asked "why" question was, "Because I'm THE MOM." Because my mother is such a strong figure, she has indelibly etched me with a set of values that play out daily in my adult life.

My mother's impact is hard to overestimate. On a regular basis, I catch myself doing things that I was trained to do, for better or for worse, and I can only imagine the number of things I do unconsciously that are like my mother. Therapy can only do so much!

My mother is a naturally meticulous and orderly person, whereas my personal inclinations are more free form and spontaneous--comparatively speaking. The family often jokes about my mother's use of the P Word: PLAN. "So what is your PLAN?" she will ask. If left to my own devices, I would make things up as I go, but I have learned to HAVE A PLAN. In my mother's eyes, lack of planning is practically a sin. Oftentimes, I feel like a sinner and a flake and a slacker for just going with the flow, even though I have not lived under her room for 20 years, and even when going with the flow is the better way to go and more in keeping with who I really am.

My mother also is a woman of high expectations for herself and others. We had a conversation the other day where I offered the platitude, "Nobody's perfect." "No," she replied, "Nobody's perfect, but I can keep on trying. Maybe I'll be perfect by the time I die!" We had a good

223

laugh over it; my mother knows herself. But I know her, too, well enough to know that there is a grain of truth in what she says. She will keep trying to be "perfect."

Certainly, the desire to be "perfect" has worn off on me, to the point where it can either drive me to excel or inhibit me from doing things where I don't have a natural aptitude. I fear doing things wrong and feel ashamed being a novice. But as my therapist often says (another authority figure in my life, and often a counterbalance), "There's nothing worth doing in life that isn't worth doing poorly." For a perfectionist, how liberating this sentiment is! I actually went and played pool recently, a game where I am very inexperienced, and I was able to enjoy myself even though I got clobbered. Believe it or not, getting clobbered and enjoying it was a step in the right direction.

As we pick up our parents' quirks, we often pick up their virtues. My mother is an amazing woman, kind, thoughtful, intelligent, funny, warm, loving, and most of all, strong. It is her strength that has been one of the greatest of her gifts. Our family went through a difficult time when my father died of suicide when I was 18 and my brother 21. Chaos and hardship engulfed the family, and the shellshock took many, many years to subside. My mother was a trooper during this time, unflagging and determined to rebuild the family. She persisted and persisted and persisted and never gave up. She always believed that there is a good life our there as long as we're willing to "do the work." She has done the work, and though I may not quite "work" in the same fashion as she does, it is her grit and willpower that I inherited from her that kept me alive and is now keeping me well.

Finally, I know my mother loves me, and this is the greatest of the gifts. Being loved by your mother, who in my case was an authority figure, has given me a sense of place in the world. Having a place in your mother's heart is to have a home. I always know that though my physical home may change or that my mother should leave this

world, the welcome mat will always be out and the cup of tea will always be ready in my mind.
By Anonymous

What have you found to be the most effective and constructive way to project authority or perform authoritative roles in both your personal and professional life?

LISTEN & LEAD
The most effective and constructive way to harness authority is to listen to people. Having said that, listening is difficult for me to do at times, as it consumes a lot of time and at times, feels like "noise." I am the kind of person who wants to move forward with an idea right away, and so incorporating disparate feedback can slow things down or complicate implementing the goal (or so I thought.) In the environment I work in, however, I have learned that unless I pay attention to everyone's point of view, the goal is lost or becomes "too much mine," and the team falls apart. Becoming a good listener was a huge struggle for me and is something I must constantly practice, and it is the cornerstone of good leadership! Plus, input is just a fact of life!

I recall a volunteer project I was working on where I was the lead with a team of twelve. Everyone had something to say, and not all of it was relevant. In addition, I was working singlehandedly on a couple of aspects of the project, and although I was "in charge," it was a volunteer project, and everyone had something to say about the work I was doing. I realized that in order to maintain leadership and have authority in the group, then I had to be open to all input. I understood that without hearing the group out, no one would be effective, and therefore, my authority would not be useful or constructive.

The project was a huge success, and afterward, there was

225

much back-slapping and glory for all. Morale stayed high, and the areas where I received input and feedback from the group were better as a result. I have learned that respecting the opinions of others through listening is the key to exercising positive authority. I wonder if next time I'll need to say anything at all, aside from, "John? You're next on the agenda..."
By NAMISD.1.6h

Neighbors

Did you ever have neighbors who turned into lifelong friends? Who were these people and what were the events that bound you together? How have you stayed in contact after you moved away?

Charles was just a neighbor at first. We lived in a subdivided house in a lovely part of San Diego called South Park. The house was built in the early 1900's and had been well cared for, save the chopped-down pepper tree in the back yard whose roots were ruining the plumbing and the soil. Charles was the owner, living in the first floor of the house, and Trevor, my boyfriend, and I had one of the two small apartments above.

Charles was tall and handsome, a blond, blue-eyed boy from Georgia with a sweet accent and an even sweeter disposition. He was a charming conversationalist, usually confining his topics to the weather, the status of the landscaping, which he was renovating, and his pug, Sassy, who never left his side. We also heard a snippet or two about Georgia Tech, where he oh-so-briefly played football. Trevor, my significant other and I, both adored him.

It wasn't long after we met Charles that Sassy died. A

very private person, Charles never really showed his grief openly, but it was obvious that he was devastated. Trevor and I brought him flowers. It was soon after that Charles' new pug, Gladys, came on the scene, her winning ways and buoyant personality taking over the neighborhood. Soon everyone knew Charles and Gladys.

Even though Charles was always surrounded by his comic pal, Gladys, there was still an air of melancholy about him. I myself at that point in life had a touch of depression and melancholy myself, and eventually, through a slowly evolving friendship, we were able to help each other.

More true to the point, the garden helped us.

The pepper tree in the back yard had been a monster. At the urging of the neighbors in the adjacent lot, the previous owner had cut it down, but it must have had acid running through its veins because nothing would grow around the stump. Charles took this as a personal affront and decided to rip it out completely and dig deep until all of the roots were removed. It was back-breaking labor, and I watched as Charles' removal project yielded a bigger and bigger pile of the offending roots.

This process took weeks, if not months, and provided ample opportunity for conversation that was no longer confined to just a few topics. I learned about the source of Charles' melancholy, and he mine.

The fun didn't really start until Charles decided to landscape the entire house. He bought an SUV and went to town. Almost every day he came home with new plants with weird Latin names, and he showed me how his design was going to come together. While he worked, I took the opportunity to read poetry, mainly Basho's haiku, which fit the spirit of the occasion. We had a ball.

When it came time for Charles to sell the house, I cannot say he was a new man or that I was a new woman, but what I can say is that we became lifelong friends. Trevor and I have since moved to a bigger, more comfortable space, but I will never forget that house or that garden. Every time Charles comes over to watch football or we have a bite to eat, I can't help but remember the days of that pepper tree and how a poisonous plant brought me one of my best friends.

By Anonymous

Husbands & Wives

Is there anything else that has happened to you or that you've experienced in this area that you would like to share?

Eight years ago our family (mom, dad, and 4 children) was turned inside out as a result of a son with a mental illness. A horrific event took place in our home where one minute we were sleeping in bed then in an instant, life changed forever. A homicide was committed as a result of a severe psychosis. That same night we moved out of our home of 10 years and never returned.

This event not only tested our marriage but it tested every family relationship that had been built over 24 years. Up to that time, my life was devoted to my entire family on many levels. Now I found myself incapable of giving to anyone other than my son with the mental illness. For two years I turned all of my energies on the realities of the crime.

Both my wife and I dealt with our new life in very different ways. In some respects we took two different paths to end up in the same place. Despite being very disconnected in our coping abilities we learned to love each other in new ways. We learned to appreciate each others pain. We learned not to have expectations. Most of

228

all, we just learned to see each other as two human beings sharing a common pain. I think we intuitively knew we could not get through it alone but we also knew we were not going to get through it the same way. Clearly my wife and I are not the same people we married. We are very fortunate that the love we shared three decades ago was able to endure and grow such that we find strength in each other.

By Anonymous

Separation & Divorce

Have you ever been in either a long-term, committed relationship or in a marriage that has endured a separation or ended in divorce? When did this happen, who was in the relationship with you, what precipitated the break, and how did it end?

The Bathtub Divorce
I was married for three years in my early twenties. My husband "Stephen" and I met in a psychiatric hospital in England. I was studying at Leeds University with UC San Diego's education abroad program. He was a nurse; I was a patient. I was in the hospital for four months, so I had time to get to know Stephen, and after I left the hospital, we dated briefly. Then, I left the country and came home, but the damage was done.

At the time, I wanted someone to take care of me. I had been diagnosed with a severe illness a year before, and I feared for my safety. I didn't know how I was going to "make it." Plus, my relationship with Stephen had a "Romeo and Juliet," forbidden quality. Infused with drama and romance, drastic measures were the norm. He wrote every day. He and his brother recorded an album for me of original songs, all about me. Then, Stephen sold everything he had, his Beatles collection, his guitars, his blood, just to put together enough money to move to the United States.

He made me feel like a million bucks.

Two months after he arrived, we got married in Vegas "for a laugh." In actuality, it wasn't fun, rather an inauspicious beginning for what was to become a topsy-turvy, roller coaster relationship.

Our marriage had many challenges, financial, political, and cultural. Although we had next to no money, Stephen liked to spend, and he was enraptured with credit cards. I was working a couple of jobs, one a little, little job, and he disrespected my work (I thought) and heedlessly bought CDs, musical equipment, expensive gifts for his family, books, anything he took a fancy to. Sometimes I worried about paying the rent on our little apartment and couldn't fathom the rising credit card bills.

Politically, he complained on and on that my family and I were too conservative and didn't "understand." As much as he loved the benefits of the American lifestyle, he didn't often want the responsibility. I began to question who had the "mental illness" because Stephen often seemed so disconnected from the "real world."

Finally, cultural communication barriers were a problem. For a Southern Californian, I am pretty direct, and oftentimes, I felt Stephen meant something besides what he was actually saying. I became frustrated on a regular basis with his inability to deal with an issue openly, when in the British culture, dealing with an issue openly, in his interpretation, was "not the done thing" or was "in bad form." The more serious the issues, the worse the obfuscation became.

Aside from our problems, Stephen and I had a lot in common. We were both artistic, high-minded, energetic, fun people. We loved to do things together and never ran out of things to talk about. He was stimulating, invigorating, and in love with life.

But as the original dynamic of the relationship began to erode, the relationship eroded with it. As my health improved, he became resentful of my independence. I became resentful of his controlling behavior.

One day he confronted me. He said, "I sacrificed everything for you, and now, I love you more than you love me."

I answered, "Yes."

This was the beginning of the "Bathtub Divorce." For about two months, I would take a bath in this big claw-footed tub that we had, and he would sit on the toilet, and we would talk about all the ways our relationship wasn't working. It was convenient that I was in the bathtub because I did a lot of crying. Tears blend.

We didn't need a lawyer. There wasn't anything to split up, really, and the only fight we had about material possessions was a passionate back and forth over a "Hothouse Flowers" CD, which I "won" and has now disappeared into the bowels of my storage unit.

My now ex-husband and I are still in touch twenty years later. We talk about 3-4 times a year, with the occasional Facebook message. He is not an American citizen, but a permanent resident. He lives in Colorado with his son, near his second ex-wife.

I am in a stable relationship of seven years with someone who is in no way like my ex-husband.

I think if there is anything to be learned from my divorce it is knowing that the relationship could have worked if I had wanted it to. In my case, the problems weren't insurmountable. Stephen is an exceptionally good person with fine qualities who has matured a great deal. Has he matured as much as me? No. Could I have kept things together? Probably.

I have also learned that patience counts for a lot in marriage--not that staying together is the answer in all relationships. Oftentimes people are too willing to "throw out the baby with the bathwater." I think that being willing to accept minute progress, "baby steps," will often pay off in the long run.

Of course, I am not sorry that things turned out the way they did. I lead a healthy and happy life with a wonderful man.

But I don't regret the past, either. I don't regret Stephen flying across the pond to start a new life with me. I don't regret getting married in Vegas. I am thankful that there are still positive feelings between me and Stephen, and I hope that what I learned from him--don't give up--will keep my chin up in difficult times.

By Anonymous

Over the years of marriage to someone suffering both chronic depression and Schizophrenia, I came to feel that as the care-giver, I too was defined by the disease. Our lives were constrained in every way by moods, crises and the expectation of limits, they were not open to possibility. Over time, and especially seeing how this impacted my children, I came to believe this required an essential dishonesty. I was not being true to who I was or could be by being a care-giver and by being limited by that. No matter how much I could love my husband and his family, I could not explore my own talents or capacities, or help my children to do that, within the confines of the diagnoses. When a sudden opportunity changed that for me, we all faced jealous rages, threats of suicide and cunning schemes to limit the opportunity. It took five years from that time to the final divorce, but I knew that it was essential to my own mental health and that of my children to take that step. One of the professionals who helped us through that process said: "It takes courage to accept that you are responsible for your own health, and cannot truly change either the health or the reality for someone else." Accepting that was the biggest challenge of the divorce.

By Anonymous

What have you learned about yourself from the divorce that you wouldn't have learned otherwise? How do you define yourself differently now?

I think it takes time to discover who you are and have become after living with mental illness and then separating from it and all of the toxicity of dealing with systems of care. I have been overwhelmed with gratitude that I did live through those years because I treasure joy and treasure the freedoms from constraint more than I ever imagined I would. As you begin to explore work and life beyond being a care-giver, or beyond the necessary survival skills, you begin to find capacities and talents you never knew you had, and you discover that some of the survival skills developed when making sure that the strange realities of the disease never contaminated the public realities of your life help enormously to keep you energetic about exploring new challenges. I know now that I do not trust or believe what most people determine as the "should's" of life, as all those kept us all in servitude to the diagnosis. I also know now that everyone of us, sick or not, must explore and engage with a diversity of challenges and opportunities. Only by doing so will we find our own pathways forward. Compassion means to have passion with someone, and we who are care-givers often take that to mean to suffer with someone. I now know it means to share vitality, to share the triumphs that come when you recognize that you, and every other person, are more than any label, and can become far more than you imagine when you begin to discover that the label is on a mere facet, not on the whole.

By Anonymous

Because of my divorce, I learned the value of "all those little things" and the value of paying attention to someone else at close range. As someone once said, "the purpose of marriage is to have a witness for the intimate details of daily life." There is something powerful about being in a relationship where someone knows your likes, your dislikes, you idiosyncrasies. It is the fact of having a "witness" that makes us feel less alone in the world, and it is the attention to little things that make us feel part of a bigger picture.

I remember after my divorce I went to Costco, somewhere I never went by myself. Costco, in my mind, was a social place, and if I was going to go, I was going to go with my husband. So there I was in Costco by myself. I went through the cheese aisle, and of course everything was in vast quantities, far too much for me. Then I saw the special, imported cheese, the huge wedge encased in black wax, and I started crying. It was "his" cheese. I was overcome by a wash of sadness and left the cart in the middle of the store and bolted out the door.

It is in fact the little things we miss, and it is easy to get forgetful in a long term relationship because all those details begin to blur. Every time I look back at my divorce, I remind myself not to let the little things slide by, but to stay awake and appreciate my significant other on an intimate level.

By Anonymous

Work & Careers

In your experience what is the single greatest determinant of a successful career? What is the most important thing you've learned about choosing your career and getting ahead?

I've learned that there is no such thing as failure, there are only results. If you don't get the result you want try something else and keep plugging. 90% of success really is just showing up - over and over and over again. I think the reason people struggle with the idea of failure is because they buy into three myths. The first is the "myth of failure." There will be thousands of times in your life when you will not get the results you hoped to. You can fail to achieve a desired or preferable result either through misguided or uninformed actions, intentional attempts at sabotage (self-induced or externally inflicted), cruel twists of fate, or the competitive efforts of an adversary. But 9 times out of 10 the reason you won't get to where you want to go is because you simply didn't know how to get there, and you got worn out trying to find the route. Ignorance and attrition are usually our greatest enemies; not malice, stupidity and incompetence. Failure is a convenient and overly reductive label that we choose to apply when we either don't want to, or can't try anymore.

There are times when you are physically prohibited from proceeding. There are times when circumstances dictate that it is prudent to suspend your efforts. There are times when it is foolish not to stop. There is nothing wrong with stopping in these situations. But most people choose to fail because they just don't want to work at something any longer or it is 'too hard'; that's just a cop out. Quitting under those conditions actually is a failure because then you've quit on yourself and you've given up on your potential to grow. Re-frame the situation in your mind. Remember, there is no such thing as failure; there are only results. If you don't like the result you get, do something different and try again. If you don't feel like pursuing your quest, then let go, but never stop because some idiot says you failed, or worse yet tells you that you are going to fail. People only say such things for one of two reasons: they're trying to make you look bad so they can feel better about themselves, or they don't understand that life is a process and that part of that process is not always getting the results you wanted. In other words, life is supposed to work that way. Failing is a precedent for learning. You're supposed to be disappointed and not always get the response you want. That's how you learn perseverance, dedication, tenacity, and that's how you develop character, ingenuity, creativity, even genius.

This leads to the second myth - the "myth of easy." There are very few things of significance in life that are truly, completely easy. Even things that seem easy have aspects that are very difficult. It's easy to love your new wife until she disagrees with you. It's easy to love your child until they refuse to do what you tell them to. American business and the media work incredibly hard to convince us that life is easy, and that you're involved with inferior products, services, or people if things aren't. We as a culture work incredibly hard to ignore all evidence to the contrary and swallow their lies hook, line and sinker because we so badly want 'easy' to be true.

We are addicted to this myth in the same way that an alcoholic is addicted to alcohol. Specifically, we make our circumstances worse by pursuing the object of our addiction. Nowhere is this more evident than in relationships. Fifty percent of all first marriages end in divorce. We become unhappy because our expectations have not been met because the relationship is not 'easy'. Using 'easy' as our measure we then begin the process of writing off the whole person because they have a component to their personality that we find difficult to deal with. We use "either – or" criteria to evaluate people, arguments and positions; meaning they EITHER have to meet all of our 'easy' criteria OR they are no good. That is a ridiculous and dangerous means of evaluation because it is so terribly oversimplified. Life, and people in particular are complex. They may have many qualities you love AND a few that you hate. The presence of one does not negate the existence of the other. Unfortunately, we run from both and refuse to work through the problematic because we shouldn't have to - after all, relationships should be easy. The more we avoid because it isn't "easy" the worse our relationships become. That's why 80% of second marriages end in divorce.

The third myth is the myth of success, completion or perfection. The male form of the success myth is being "finished", "done" or "having arrived." The ultimate embodiment of this myth is becoming a Partner, getting the CEO job or corner office; owning the car, house or yacht you always wanted; or never having to leave the golf course. The female version of the myth deals with perfection, and is embodied by the perfect dress, figure, wedding, husband, home, kids, etc. The myth of success is in many ways more insidious than the myth of failure. While many of us learn to get past our perceived failures, few of us ever really stop wiping ourselves to achieve 'success'. The danger with this myth is that we obsess so completely on obtaining our dream that we ignore everything else in life. One of the most tragic examples of this I ever witnessed came from the Partner who hired me at this "Big Four" accounting firm. I was attending the annual Christmas party and my date and I were seated next to this man and his wife. The mood even at the outset of the evening was somewhat strained between the two of them, but it rapidly deteriorated as the night went on and she had a few drinks. As I was seated to the immediate left of my boss's wife I quickly learned the cause for her simmering disgust for her soon to be ex-husband. It turned out that shortly after he had joined PW she had given birth to a daughter. They soon discovered that the girl had been born deaf. She was now 15. In all those years he had been so wrapped up in trying to "make Partner" that he never had time to learn sign language. He could not communicate with his own child unless others in the family translated. It has been over 20 years since that evening and I still internally recoil in horror even telling the story. The irony of this man's fate was that after his wife left him and took every status

237

symbol he had accumulated he also lost his position at PW and was financially ruined. Working for a goal is fine, but don't do it to the exclusion of all else in your life.

Success is not an event or state that you achieve; it is a process that you embrace. Finished only happens when you die. Perfect is only found in things that you have zero control over, and can't hope to create like a sunset, a wave, or the view from the Eastern Sierras. Like failure, success is only a result. However, in this case one that more closely aligns with your desires and expectations. Results in turn are only milestones that we reach after effort, sacrifice or pure luck. Once we reach these milestones and instantly pass them by, we realize that this isn't our destination but rather a bend in the curve around which the next milestone comes into view. Be sure to celebrate the milestones, but keep them in perspective. Be happy when things go well, but live your life so that you have people to be happy with. Remember that life is an ultra-marathon. You can't run this race like you do a 100-meter sprint. If you don't live the process of life successfully, you can never sustain the results you're hoping to achieve. The secret of success isn't so much to 'get there' as it is to get there by the right road. You cannot reach a truly good destination if you take a bad road to get there. You have to give up too much of your soul along the way.
By Anonymous

A few years ago I would have said timing or being at the right place at the right time and being reasonably well prepared when the right time presents itself. I have had multiple experiences where I have either made a lot of money or missed a lot of money by either fortuitously being in the right place and making the right call or not being ready to go when the call came. I watched the same thing happen to a lot of other very capable people. I've learned that it's much better to be lucky than smart, and I've learned that often the wealthiest people or those in the highest positions within organizations are often not the smartest. I've also learned that what these people do tend to have is an ability to understand and work with people. These people tend to understand the importance of relationships.

My thinking has changed so much on this issue that now I'd say it's really all about relationships and coordinating the talents of the people you are in relationship with to achieve the objectives you are trying to reach. Business is about people. People do business with people they like. They avoid people they don't like. It's really that simple. If you can't get along with people; if you can't appreciate the unique strengths that everyone brings to the table, then you're never going to be able to assemble the right team around you so that you can be successful. None of us has all the skills we need to get everything done in our increasingly complex, increasingly project oriented economy. We need each other in business and in life. The people who realize that and embrace it are the ones who are the most successful.

You can be the smartest guy in the world, you can be incredibly technically proficient at your job, but if you're dishonest, a jerk (and that is a polite way to cover a wide range of offensive behaviors), or can't appreciate the value that others bring to the table no one is going to want to work with you once they figure you out. A good mask can initially fool a lot people, but in the long run if your appreciation and respect for others is not authentic, you're dead.
By NAMISD.2020

Leadership

What do you know about leadership today that you wish you had known before you led people? What should every leader know before they are put in charge?

239

Most people act like sheep because they don't want to look foolish. A good leader isn't afraid to take a risk and have it not work out. The next time you're in a theatre or auditorium and are walking out look for the double doors at the exit. Invariably one of the doors is open and the other closed. People will be lined up 50 deep in front of the open door waiting patiently (and sometimes impatiently) to get out. All the while the other door sits closed - with no one even trying to open it! When you see this, make a point of going up to the closed door and trying to open it. Nine times out of ten it will be unlocked and you'll burst right through. Ten percent of the time the door will be locked and you'll have to go to the back of the line. If that happens, so what, but if it opens, notice how fast people fall in line behind you to go through the newly opened door.

People are afraid to blaze new trials because they don't want to be embarrassed if things don't work out. They play it safe and wait in line to avoid looking stupid. How ridiculous! You'll never know if something works unless you try. A real leader doesn't worry about looking stupid. They're much less concerned with ego than results.
By Anonymous

Stewardship & Charitable Donations

What is the relationship between your generosity or impulse to give and your sense of gratitude? For what are you grateful?

Above all I am grateful for life, and for the ability to share life with others. I have an overwhelming sense of being part of a whole, and that as others have helped and supported me at times in my life, so it is my turn to share who I am and what I have with others, that is how the whole works and that is why it has meaning. I do not mean that there is any transaction--if I give this, I will get that back--rather I mean that we are all making music together, each in our own way. We may not hear the whole of this symphony, but we can bend to the rhythms and know that as we hear the songs of others, so our song is heard. My father was a fragile invalid for most of my childhood and we expected death at the dinner table every night; my husband was suicidal and in mental anguish most of my marriage; so I am daily astonished by joy and grateful to know that my sons laugh and explore living wholeheartedly. We are so much more than we think we are, and capable of far greater contribution than we ever imagine, I think generosity is an expression of gratitude in every way.

By Anonymous

How have decisions you've made about stewardship and charitable giving impacted your life?

Once I made the decision to live my life with a focus on gratitude, my life became an incredibly exciting adventure. I have encountered astonishing people and been part of world-changing efforts for good as a result of this, but the choice is to be grateful for each day. I think that emerging from the constraints of care-giving and the draining sense of responsibility required when living with mental illness has really been an emergence into joy.

Life has not been easy, and there have been many times when I could have chosen financial stability instead of living in gratitude, but I know that I would not have the sense of wonder had I not chosen this path. Being a good friend takes work and awareness and commitment and patience and all those things with discipline, but the result is so much more than any one of those virtues. So too, being a steward of life and of the lives I encounter requires dedication and discipline and other seemingly hard things, but it is an adventure releasing vitality.

I think the choice to live in gratitude is really a choice to embrace life and a constant journey of discovery. I also believe it becomes a sacred journey. You do not know where you are going, but you know that you must continue and you are supported by the love and faith and hope that you share with others on the way. There is no disease, and no label, which diminishes our capacities to make this choice and take this journey.
By Anonymous

Faith, Beliefs & Religion

What do you believe? Who is your God, and what is he or she like? Who or what is the Lord of your life, and what is your relationship with him, her or it?

I believe that Jesus Christ suffered and died for our sins. Our family has suffered great losses and tragedy as a result of a son living with mental illness. I have had to endure experiences that have changed my family in profound and painful ways. My God gives me the ability to somehow make sense of tragedy. I have come to terms with the fact that my grieving is life long however through my faith I realize there is a purpose for my grief. I and my family are not the first, nor will we be the last to live in pain. Jesus and his family teach us this. I have learned that through Christ's example, much good can come from pain when it is put into perspective. Without my faith the pain would be impossible to live with. My faith allowed me not to be angry with God rather it helped me to know him better.
By Anonymous

What is the core or most fundamental belief that you cling to in times of trouble?

Jesus Christ died for us and his family suffered tremendously. We too can live with pain and suffering on our journey for eternal life.
By NAMISD.1.1b

How does your faith equip you to live and how does it prepare you to die?

The most valuable "learned lesson" gift I would like to share is the importance of belief in a power larger than ourselves. That power may be called by many names, but down to my core, this belief has guided me and shaped me throughout my life. Often I have been asked, "how can you believe in something you cannot see?" My answer may not work for everyone, but I have a solid sense of well being that God is with me and in me. I have had many challenges throughout life and it is with this belief I have survived.

As a young girl, I learned to talk to him, much as a friend, and though loneliness and difficult family situations threatened my very interest in living, God sustained me, through prayer and also through bringing people into my world to help me understand myself, love myself, and find value in my life and living. As the darkness of depression enveloped me as a young woman, God was always with me and frequently whispered.."hang on, I am here, you are not alone." I realized God couldn't keep me from these challenges, but through these times, I learned I was strong and I was a survivor.

From this core value of faith, I believe another lesson for life becomes apparent. That belief is that our gift back to God is to make it our life's work to understand and use our strengths and talents. This understanding may not

243

always be apparent, but again placing trust in your higher power, those gifts will present themselves. It is my impression very few of us are born with a keen understanding of our talents and place in this world. Not all will enjoy the challenge and work of this, but if you do, the sheer joy of understanding and utilizing your God given talents is nothing short of exhilirating and life changing.

My third gift "lesson" to others is again something I learned at a young age and has sustained me thoughout my life. That lesson is trying to interact with and love the "difficult and irregular" people that become a part of our world. I believe if we constantly remind ourselves that people are usually doing the best they can with the tools they were given in life, we can often find empathy for most people. Not all of us had a complete and hardy "tool bag" to move through life. If I start with that belief I can bring kindness and compassion to all that I meet.
By NAMISD.1.3h

Self-Destructive & Addictive Behaviors

What do you want others to know about addictions? What do you know today that you wish you had known on the day you realized you were addicted?

At it's core every psychological addiction is nothing more than an attempt to kill pain. Addictions often start as a seemingly rationale attempt just to function. This may or may not be a healthy coping mechanism from the outset, but it usually becomes unhealthy quickly. The thing to which the person becomes addicted is originally the solution to a problem. Unfortunately, the solution becomes the problem and then you've got two problems to deal with.

The exact same holds true with mental illness. Those with an illness start self-medicating to mask the pain and deaden the voices in their head (whether figurative or literal). But then the voices creep back in, and more of the 'solution' is required to achieve the original effect. From this point on it's all down hill - fast. The only way to break an addiction is to completely cut off or discontinue any use or interaction with the addictive substance or behavior. That means confronting the pain head on, sometimes without much hope of ever having that pain go away.
By Anonymous

Identity & Self-Perception

Is there anything else that has happened to you or that you've experienced in this area that you would like to share?

Growing up I never liked myself, especially during my teenager years. When I was diagnosed Bi-Polar, things took a downward spiral. I felt judged all the time, that I was crazy and insane. My self-image was extremely low, and I had no sense of my identity. I am 21 years old now, and attempted suicide three times, once at 15, 17, and 19 years old. I was unable to accept the fact that I was Bi-Polar, and that it was a part of me. Also make note that during these times I was struggling with drug addiction and alcoholism. I didn't have to live with a label floating above my head all the time, but I hated that I had an ailment of that nature. This last time around I had my former support group step in and they gave me a reality check, that if I continued trying to kill myself I would end up a ward of the state and they would have control of my life. I decided that I DID NOT want that, and started letting the people around me help me.

By Kia426

Are there any other things that you have learned about this topic that you would like to share with us? What are we not asking you, that we should be asking you, if we knew to ask it?

You will find in your life what you choose to see in your life. A while back I attended the most heart-wrenching memorial I have ever witnessed, but it was not difficult for reasons one might expect. The service was for a 17 & ½ year-old boy with Down's syndrome who had died unexpectedly in his sleep the Sunday morning before. The service began with the Pastor reading a letter from the family's 1998 Christmas card. The letter, obviously ghost written by one of the parents from the first person perspective of the boy, then 8, chronicled his life as the second child of the family from his birth to that date. The tone of the letter was noteworthy for it's simplicity, innocence, complete lack of self-pity, and the message written between the lines, the one that no one in the gathering of 750 people could miss - the celebration of the purity of love.

This child endured 30 operations over the course of his life. The first one coming when he was just 6 hours old. For all the nightmares and brushes with death that he and their family had encountered over the years, their focus was never on the hardship, but rather on the ways they had gotten through. And more importantly on how their lives had benefited by the struggle.

As the pastor concluded and the father rose to deliver the eulogy my heart ached for this guy I'd known casually for about 20 years. I could not imagine the living hell he was feeling at that moment; and could not fathom whether I could be so poised if I were delivering the eulogy for one of my two kids. As he spoke he reinforced the message set in their Christmas letter of 9 years before. This child had not been, as I and others would have by reflex supposed, been a horrible burden. To the contrary, the innocence of his love, the purity of his spirit and his utter lack of malice had evidently been one of the greatest gifts they had ever experienced in their life. This family was not relieved that a heartbreaking situation and terrible burden had been removed from them. They were devastated to the last family member that this great love and been taken away from them. I would have given anything if the service could have been video recorded so that it could have been played back for every young couple who just found out that they had given birth to a Down's baby. What we from such a selfish perspective often view as a defect, I think God must see as a great opportunity. I know that sounds like some sort of Jesus Freak Pollyanna glossing over the horrible, but this child's life and his presence in their family wasn't horrible for these people. It was one of the greatest things that ever happened to them, and like I said everyone at the service got the message.

When was the last time you heard of 750 people attending the memorial of somebody whose life was a mistake? When was the last time you walked away from a memorial with an object lesson that nobody was trying to make it just screamed at you from the sentiment of the moment? When was the last time you felt ashamed that you had so badly missed the real point of life because you had mentally written off something or someone that didn't measure up to your expectations? The perfect doesn't exist in human form, and yet we spend so much time trying to either convince ourselves or pretend that it does. Choosing to love, embrace and accept the imperfect in each other is infinitely better, infinitely more real, and infinitely more important than clinging to the myth of perfection our society is constantly shoving down our throat.

By Anonymous

Your Actions & Self-Determination

Are there any other things that you have learned about this topic that you would like to share with us? What are we not asking you, that we should be asking you, if we knew to ask it?

The only person you can control in this life is you. You can't control anybody or anything other than you. Said differently, the only person you can control in this life is you. The only thing you can control is how you respond to the things that happen to you. The sooner you embrace these truths at a cellular level the better off and happier you'll be. Nobody can make you feel anything. You chose how you will respond, what you will feel, and how you will act. You should never surrender that power to anyone else - ever.
By Anonymous

Changing, Growth & Adaptation

What is the most significant change, or the most significant periods of change that you have experienced in your life? What brought these changes on, why were they so significant, and what were the consequences of the change?

The most significant period change in my life happened most recently. As an attorney of 10+ years, you tend to see all kinds of crazy things - clients that want to bend the rules "just once," as well as other clients that sincerely wish that the other side would "just die." It can be sad, but at least I have the opportunity to counsel such clients through their most trying times; at least that is how I felt until recently.

No more than two months ago I was faced with the issue of two trials starting at the same time. For most of you who are unaware, I would equate trial preparation similar to that of preparing for your very worst college final - you know what you need to study to do well, but there is just way too much to complete in too short of time. Well, I had two staring back at me with no option to allow one to be delayed over the other. On top of that, both clients had recently informed me that they were having financial difficulties and didn't believe that they were going to be able to pay the remainder of the services necessary to protect them.

As you could imagine, this was a problem for me in that the wonderful judicial system "protects" the interests of clients in that the Court does not allow attorneys to remove themselves from cases they are not getting paid on within 3 months of the trial date. Needless to say, I was not only facing mountains of work, I was also facing the issue that I would have to perform the work for free! Oh, did I mention that I run my own law firm and that working on these two trials for the next two months, for free, was a formula for business failure.

My back was against the wall. For the last few months I had been trying to reach a common sense settlement for each of my clients. Both clients wanted nothing to do with the suggestion of settlement as it was a matter of principle and "why should they have to give in?" I had tried to explain a number of times that litigation is just another phase of business negotiations and that getting tied up in the emotions of it all will only lead to another bad business decision. All of the rationale was disregarded, so I began preparing for each trial.

249

As each day passed I became more and more concerned as to the outcome of each of my clients' cases as well as the outcome of my law firm. I was going into the office at 5:30 am and leaving at 9 pm. I thought by putting in long hours that I could control the outcome. That was a lesson I was about to learn was not so.

I started every morning praying and asking God to give me the strength to get through the day and help open the eyes of the parties engaged in the litigation. I also had my wife and mom doing the same. While it did not appear at that time that the prayers were working, it gave me comfort to know that my Maker was listening. However, as each day went by without an answer I began to try and control matters more and more. While I had thought that I was being faithful, I was acting quite the opposite. Each evening I would come home to my wife, dump all my frustrations on her and refuse to listen to her solid advice that I needed to have faith that things (that were out of my hands) would turn out for the best. She held strong to her message until I finally relented.

With two weeks left before each trial date I walked into the "disaster zone" otherwise known as my office. It was obvious from my perspective that I had no control and that it was time to rely entirely on God. That same afternoon, a break in one of my cases happened. I received a call from the opposing attorney asking me whether my client would consider settling. After hearing the terms of the settlement offer I was most certain that the case was heading for trial. Moments later I conveyed the offer to my client and they were receptive to the offer and wanted to counter with terms that I found to be overwhelmingly reasonable. After several rounds of talks, the matter was settled! I was down to only one case. It was wild, I let go of control just for a moment and something I thought was absolutely impossible happened within a few hours time. With one last case to focus upon I went back to trying to control the outcome. For days I spoke with my client about the shortcomings in the case and the need to soften up to a settlement offer. The client would have nothing to do with it. My client was aware that I was stuck in this trial (regardless of payment) and was ready to play out her personal vendetta to the bitter end. As the week began to wind down I reminded myself that I had no control; that I had to be prepared to the best of my ability; but that the results were out of my hands. Three days before the start of a two month trial the parties buried the hatchet.

While I may face a rough road to recovery, financially, I have learned a number of life lessons along the way. First, never disregard the loving words of your spouse. They are right beside you suffering and when you don't allow any weight to their words it breaks their heart. I hope to never undervalue the support of my wife ever again. She is the most important person in the world and she should be appreciated always.

Second, attempting to control the outcome of matters that are out of your hands is pointless and causes unnecessary stress that interferes with time you could be spending on other useful matters. Whether it be controlling the outcome of a settlement or something as meaningful as a job search, you can only control matters that are in your hands. Always apply your best efforts and then have faith. I have never been disappointed with the outcome. I may have been disappointed through portions of the process, but the outcome has always been the best result. There are many more lessons that came out of this experience but some I am still trying to hash out. This life experience was horrible (and continues to be financially), but the lessons have been priceless.

By counselbg

Triumphs & Tragedies

How have you kept yourself going after either a great gain or a terrible loss? How have you kept these events from destroying you and your family? How have you answered the questions 'why me', 'why us', 'why now'?

I ask myself what have I to learn from this experience? What insights can I share with others that will help others avoid the same fate or help them heal from their own experience? For example, I have attempted to take the process of contributing to this book very seriously. I wanted to do a very good job of it, but other people were telling me that it wasn't worth the stress I was imposing on myself. I told them I disagree. I believe that other people will be coming down this road after me and maybe they can learn something from me and my experience that would help them live a more meaningful life. If that's the case, then it would make some of my experiences more worthwhile. I would like to give the people who will follow the tools to live a more meaningful life.

By Anonymous

The End

Made in the USA
Lexington, KY
19 January 2011